CHERNOBYL

The Ongoing Story of the World's Deadliest Nuclear Disaster

GLENN ALAN CHENEY

A TIMESTOP BOOK

New Discovery Books
New York

Maxwell Macmillan Canada
Toronto

Maxwell Macmillan International
New York Oxford Singapore Sydney

For the children

· ·

Photo Credits
AP-Wide World Photos: 14–15, 41, 42, 57, 87, 88, 91, 94, 96, 100
Vladimir Savran: 21, 49
Glenn Alan Cheney: 63, 66, 71, 113, 114, 117

New Discovery Books
Macmillan Publishing Company
866 Third Avenue
New York, NY 10022

Maxwell Macmillan Canada, Inc.
1200 Eglinton Avenue East
Suite 200
Don Mills, Ontario M3C 3N1

Macmillan Publishing Company is part of the Maxwell Communication Group of Companies.

First Edition

Printed in the United States of America

10 9 8 7 6 5 4 3 2 1

Library of Congress Cataloging-in-Publication Data

Cheney, Glenn Alan.
    Chernobyl, the ongoing story of the world's deadliest nuclear disaster / by Glenn Alan Cheney. — 1st ed.
       p. cm.
    Includes bibliographical references (p.) and index.
    Summary: Examines in depth the 1986 explosion, the subsequent coverup by the Soviet government, and the continuing health problems it caused.
    ISBN 0-02-718305-X
    1. Chernobyl Nuclear Accident, Chernobyl, Ukraine, 1986—Juvenile literature. 2. Chernobyl Nuclear Accident, Chernobyl, Ukraine, 1986—Health aspects—Juvenile literature. [1. Chernobyl Nuclear Accident, Chernobyl, Ukraine, 1986. 2. Nuclear power plants—Accidents.] I. Title.
TK1362.S65C46 1993
363.17'99'0947714—dc20   93-17508

Contents

Introduction

The explosion that destroyed Number Four Reactor at the Chernobyl nuclear power plant on April 26, 1986, was the biggest accident in history. It rendered an area the size of New York State unsafe for human habitation. It left a city of 42,000 people abandoned for the next 500 years. It killed 31 people almost immediately. Within the next few years, the Soviet government admitted the deaths of 224 others. The actual toll, however, is probably several thousand. In the next few years, the number may reach the tens of thousands. Lingering radiation is causing uncountable thousands of people to suffer an immune deficiency syndrome and mysterious new forms of disease. Among a population of millions, it contributes to a death rate that now exceeds the birth rate.

Ironically, despite the size of the accident, no one knows exactly what happened or why, who is to blame, how many have died, who is still suffering, or whether a similar accident, or several, might happen again. Explanations are as varied as the motivations behind them. Governments are blaming one another for cover-ups and incompetence. Mothers accuse governments of murder. Former Soviet bureaucrats accuse mothers of hysteria. Scientists contradict one another. Doctors try to link radiation, pollution, and malnutrition to explain a syndrome similar to AIDS. Measurements of radiation seem to depend on who does the measuring. Some environmentalists claim to have identified biological damage on the other side of the globe. The United Nations International Atomic Energy Agency, on the other hand, has declared the world free of aftereffects. The United Nations World Health Organization, however, has found soaring rates of cancer in the Chernobyl area.

Some historians suggest that the accident was the final blow to the empire of the Soviet Union. The largest country in the world, the Soviet Union was already staggering under economic collapse, corruption, incompetence, political paranoia, and unwieldy bureaucracy. All these forces came into focus at Chernobyl on April 26, 1986. A poorly designed reactor built to substandard specifications was manned by incompetent technicians and allowed to operate without any of its emergency protection systems. Then, after the explosion, bureaucratic, political, and economical considerations caused the full scope of the accident to be hidden, exposing millions to needlessly high doses of radiation.

The Soviet leader at that time, Mikhail Gorbachev, apparently recognized that the accident had resulted from and symbolized all that was ill with his country. For the first time in Soviet history, the government admitted to a major failure. To the surprise of the world, Gorbachev began to take corrective action. Critics of the Soviet system were allowed to speak out without fear of punishment. Scientists were allowed to share data with Western countries, the Soviet Union's former enemies. The Communist party relinquished its total control of the government. The Soviet empire could not hold up against the truth and freedom. One by one, the Soviet republics declared their independence from the central government in Moscow. In December 1991, five and a half years after the accident, the independent states joined in a loosely defined "sovereignty." The Chernobyl power plant then fell under the authority of a new country called Ukraine.

Only now is some of the truth being brought to light. Nuclear technicians are revealing what really happened on the day of the explosion. Families are speaking out about the deadly neglect they suffered in the aftermath. The 600,000 workers who tried to clean up the radioactive mess have formed a union and are discovering how many of them have died or are dying. Doctors are gathering statistics that show a startling and horrifying deterioration of health in Ukraine and Belarus. Journalists are investigating the situation. New political leaders are exposing, and sometimes exaggerating, official evidence of what really happened.

Chernobyl is not old news. The world has seen only the beginning of the tragedy. The death toll is still rising. The diseases are growing worse. While no one has a viable plan for cleaning up the ruins of the reactor, radioactive fuel is slowly leaking into the ground and air. There still exists the possibility of the remaining fuel reaching critical mass and exploding in an atomic chain reaction. Most horrifying of all, 40 other reactors of the Chernobyl type are still operating in eastern Europe and the former Soviet states. In 25 other countries, 426 atomic power plants continue to operate.

It is important to understand the causes and consequences of Chernobyl. The causes show us some of what was wrong with the Soviet Union. The consequences show us the potential danger of working with nuclear power.

CHAPTER ONE

. . . .

An Accident Waiting to Happen

T he nuclear reactors at Chernobyl—four were operating in
1986—are of a type known as RBMK, a Russian acronym meaning
Large Power Boiling Reactor. The RBMK generates electricity by
heating water. The water turns to steam which, expanding under
pressure, forces the blades of a turbine to turn. Each reactor
powers two turbines.

The heat comes from an atomic chain reaction. Neutrons
thrown off from radioactive elements—in this case the uranium
fuel—smash into similar atoms nearby. These atoms break up,
releasing energy and more neutrons. These neutrons go on to
break up more atoms and release more energy. It happens very
quickly, and the release of energy is far more than that of mere
fire. A pound of uranium 235 can produce the heat energy of 1,500
tons of coal. The Number Four Reactor at Chernobyl was loaded
with 185 tons of uranium 235.

The core of the RBMK reactor, a cylinder 46 feet (14 meters)
in diameter and 23 feet (7 meters) tall, consists of stacks of
nuclear fuel assemblies packed within columns of graphite. Each
column also has a channel into which a control rod can be low-

ered. The rods, made of boron carbide, absorb the free neutrons that shoot out from decaying uranium fuel. The more control rods in place, the fewer the electrons continuing the chain reaction. If all 211 control rods are in place, the reactor stops reacting. If none or not enough are in place, the reactor is not unlike a very large atomic bomb.

The explosion at Chernobyl, however, was not an atomic explosion. It was a steam explosion followed, probably, by a chemical explosion. It happened during an experiment.

The operators of the plant wanted to see what would happen during a blackout. The plant ran on electricity tapped off the national power grid. It needed this electricity to power everything from the light bulbs to the motors that raised and lowered the control rods. If the plant failed to receive the electric power, it would have to be shut down immediately. If it wasn't, and if the auxiliary diesel generators failed to supply enough power to the plant, electric water pumps would not be able to circulate the water needed to cool the core. The core would quickly heat to its own melting point. Becoming a white-hot miniature sun, it would destroy the structure around it as it burned its way through the floor and into the earth, the famous "China Syndrome." But it wouldn't literally burn its way through to the other side of the earth. As soon as it hit the underground water table, it would explode in a monstrous burst of superheated steam.

The problem with stopping the nuclear reaction during a blackout would be that the plant needed electricity to perform its shutdown procedures.

Theoretically the spinning turbines could continue to generate electric power under their own inertia as they gradually slowed. But would the power last long enough to lower the control rods, cool the reactor, and take the other complex steps necessary to stop the reactor? There was only one way to find out.

Who Was (and Wasn't) in Charge?

The director of the Chernobyl nuclear power plant, V. P. Bryukhanov, was not a specialist in nuclear energy. His specialty was turbines. His experience and training were in a coal-fired power plant. Likewise, his chief engineer, Nikolai Fomin, came directly from a conventional power plant to Chernobyl. Anatoly Dyatlov, deputy chief engineer of Reactors Three and Four, had some experience with small nuclear reactors but had not dealt with the intricacies of a large reactor.

Soviet regulations required nuclear plant directors to request permission to perform tests and experiments. Theoretically, the plan would be analyzed and approved by the Gidroproyekt ("Hydroproject") Institute, which oversaw the design of the plant; Soyuzatomenergo ("Atomic Energy Agency"), the Ministry of Energy department responsible for plant personnel and activities; and the Nuclear Safety Committee, which had authority to shut down nuclear power facilities if they failed to meet safety standards. Unfortunately, Gidroproyekt and Soyuzatomenergo were headed by directors who had never been trained in nuclear physics or the complexities of nuclear power plants.

In January 1986, Bryukhanov submitted his request and plan. When he failed to receive an answer, he thought nothing of it. That was the way the Soviet bureaucracy worked. Bureaucrats, protective of their jobs and fearful of excessive punishment if they did something wrong, figured the safest thing to do was to do nothing. The best decision was no decision. A good bureaucrat followed orders and volunteered nothing extra.

The bureaucrats may also have been unaware that nuclear accidents could take place. When accidents occurred—and they occurred frighteningly often—they were kept secret. The plant designers at Gidroproyekt would not know what someone at Soyuzatomenergo knew about a weakness in the system. The Nuclear Safety Committee would not inform all plant engineers about accidents at other plants. Unless an engineer or operator witnessed an accident firsthand, he or she would assume that the safety systems worked perfectly.

So neither director Bryukhanov nor chief engineer Fomin were surprised when the central government agencies did not reply to their request to perform an experiment. Confident in their safety systems, they decided to go ahead with their plan.

Safety Second

In retrospect, the Chernobyl power plant was doomed to disaster. It was poorly designed, poorly constructed, and poorly managed by poorly trained engineers.

The poor construction of the plant was not a secret at the time of the accident. Just a month earlier, a lengthy article published in a newspaper in Pripyat, the nearby city built for the Chernobyl workers, cited several construction flaws. Years later, a release of KGB documents revealed that the government knew of many flaws and problems. Some of the flaws resulted from the government's rush to bring the plant on-line. When the builders encountered a problem, they often went ahead with construction, however shoddy. Key parts that had to be perfectly level were off by as much as three degrees. When suppliers failed to deliver enough cement, builders simply added more sand. Many metal components were defective. For the radioactive waste deposi-

The Chernobyl nuclear power plant

tory, builders installed 326 tons of defective steel sheathing and 220 tons of defective pillars to hold it up.

As it happened, these flaws made no difference in the performance of the Number Four Reactor. It blew up before they could

cause an accident. The fear today throughout the former Soviet Union is that dozens of other reactors were built with the same shoddy craftsmanship.

As if the substandard construction were not enough to doom the reactor, the design of the plant allowed operators to switch off all safety systems.

All nuclear reactors have several built-in emergency protection systems. When something goes wrong—a blackout, an earthquake, the failure of a water pump, an excessive temperature, an escape of radioactivity—the systems automatically take corrective action. They may switch to an alternate source of electricity or water coolant. They may reduce the rate of atomic reaction. They may shut down the reactor altogether.

The RBMK reactor at Chernobyl had several main safety systems. When an emergency was detected, an emergency power-reduction system would go into action. All 211 graphite control rods would lower into the fuel assembly columns. Emergency diesel generators would start up to provide auxiliary power. Auxiliary water pumps would switch on to increase the flow of water to the reactor. The emergency core cooling system (ECCS) would feed in more water via a different route. Yet another emergency supply of water would flow in from a pressurized tank.

Most other types of reactors have similar (and additional) emergency systems, but they are designed so that they cannot be shut off. Furthermore, they are connected to a single "design-failure" button. If, in the event of a failure in the designed structure of the facility, this button is tripped, all safety systems go into action. Under no circumstances could all the systems, and especially the design-failure button, be shut off or bypassed.

In the RBMK reactor system, it was possible to disconnect all the safety systems. On top of that, the design-failure button, which had been installed just two weeks before the accident, operated through the backup diesel generators. If the generators were not operating, the button was useless. Even if the button was working, an operator would have to hold it down for up to a minute, preventing him or her from taking other action elsewhere during the emergency.

The test conducted on April 26, 1986, was to see if the turbines could produce electricity if the reactor was no longer powering them. In a similar test conducted earlier, the turbines continued to turn long enough, but they did not supply sufficient power to shut the reactor down. In that experiment, however, not all safety systems were disconnected.

Chernobyl director Bryukhanov and chief engineer Fomin wanted to conduct a "pure" experiment. "Pure" meant simulating emergency conditions as much as possible. Since the simulated blackout was an emergency situation, the diesel generators had to be disconnected. Otherwise they would automatically begin replacing the electricity that was no longer arriving from the outside power grid.

The plan also called for the disconnection of the emergency power reduction system. The justification was that if the reactor overheated, emergency water would automatically feed in to cool it. The result, however, might be like that of taking crockery from a hot oven and plunging it into cold water. The thermal shock would damage or even destroy the reactor. Apparently the engineers assumed they could cool the reactor in other ways. They seemed to think an overheated nuclear reactor was no more serious than an overheated coal-fired boiler, that it could just be switched off and cooled down.

All of this was part of the technical plan submitted to the authorities in Moscow. Presumably, a plan calling for the operation of a nuclear power plant without any safety systems would have been disapproved rather than approved. For some mysterious reason, however, the bureaucracy did neither, and the experiment went ahead as planned.

The Explosion

The test was originally scheduled for April 25. At 1:00 P.M. on that day, Anatoly Dyatlov, deputy engineer for Reactors Three and Four, ordered the reduction of power at Reactor Four. Normally it operated at 3,000 megawatts (MW) of thermal power. When the power level reached 1,600 MW, Turbogenerator Number Seven (one of two powered by Reactor Four) was switched off. It no longer fed into the general power grid that supplied Ukraine and other areas with electricity. Turbogenerator Number Eight, the center of the forthcoming experiment, continued to run off the reactor power and to supply the grid and the reactor complex with electricity.

At 2:00 P.M., as scheduled, engineers disconnected the emergency core cooling system. Though part of the plan, this action was a clear violation of all national and international safety rules.

Moments later, an electrical dispatcher in Kiev requested that the test be postponed until after midnight. The demand for electricity would be lower then. The engineers at Chernobyl agreed to wait. The reactor continued to run at 50 percent power—about 1,500 MW—and to turn Turbogenerator Number Eight.

At 11:00 that night, operators resumed the programmed

power reduction. The test was to begin when the power level stabilized between 700 and 1,000 MW.

Seven hundred megawatts was the minimum power level per-
mitted in an RBMK reactor. Above that level, the reactor achieves
a natural balance between two opposing forces. The presence of
cooling water in the core tends to slow the rate of reaction, or
reactivity. As the water changes to steam, the reactivity increases.
The higher the reactivity, the higher the heat. The higher the
heat, the more steam produced, which in turn further raises reactivity.

An opposing force counterbalances this self-feeding cycle.
Reactivity decreases as the nuclear fuel becomes hotter. The
reduced reactivity lowers the temperature, which in turn reduces
the amount of steam produced, which therefore increases the
amount of cooling water, which therefore further reduces the
reactivity.

As long as the reactor runs at over 700 MW, these forces tend
to balance each other. Below that level, however, the reactor
becomes unstable and hard to control. A system called a local
automatic control is designed to either maintain that level or shut
the reactor down. To prevent a shutdown during the experiment,
the local automatic control was disconnected.

Without the automatic control, the operators were unable to
maintain the proper power level. It fell to 30 MW. The low reactivity caused the fuel to produce abnormally high levels of iodine isotopes. These isotopes began to contaminate the fuel, making it
very difficult to increase power again. The engineers were faced
with the choice of shutting down the reactor or raising the power
level. If they shut down the reactor, they would not be able to perform their test on Turbogenerator Number Eight. Since the reac-

tor was due to be shut down for routine maintenance, they would have to wait a full year before they could try again.

On duty at the time were the senior reactor control engineer, Leonid Toptunov, and the shift foreman, Aleksandre Akimov. Deputy Chief Engineer Dyatlov ordered Toptunov and Akimov to pull out more control rods and raise the power level high enough to perform the test on Turbogenerator Number Eight.

At first, Toptunov refused. Regulations required at least 28 control rods in place. He knew the danger of removing more. But he also knew the consequences of disobeying an order. A young man—he was only 26—he did not dare stand up to his superior. He followed the order, pulling out control rods one by one, gradually "burning off" some of the iodine 131 and other isotopes that result from nuclear reaction. Power gradually increased, and the reactor stabilized at 200 MW.

But with only 18 rods now lowered into the core, the reactor was highly unstable. Shutting it down would be extremely difficult. Nonetheless, in defiance of the facility's own safety rules, the emergency core cooling system was left disconnected, and operators proceeded to prepare the reactor system for the test.

At 1:03 A.M., operators started two additional pumps and increased the flow of water to the reactor. The purpose was to keep the reactor cool as Turbogenerator Number Eight wound down. But this increased the flow of water through the core, which resulted in a lowering of steam production, which resulted in lower power production. Operators compensated by pulling out even more control rods. Meanwhile, the lack of steam in other parts of the system forced operators to increase the flow of water, which put too much pressure on the pumps.

The reactor could not have been in a more precarious situation. Power was unstable and at a level far below the permissible. The nuclear fuel was still contaminated by iodine and other isotopes. The number of control rods in the core was far below the permissible. Water pumps were running beyond their capacity. The reactor trigger connected to the turbogenerators was neutralized. The triggers linked to water level (which was too high) and steam pressure (which was too low) were neutralized, as was the trigger linked to heat levels. The emergency core cooling system was turned off. And the whole thing was built so poorly that it hardly needed the help of incompetent engineers to self-destruct.

Nonetheless, at 1:23 A.M., the reactor seemed stable enough for the test to begin. Under orders of Director Bryukhanov, opera-

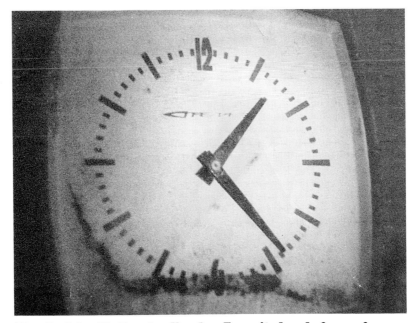

The clock inside Reactor Number Four, its hands frozen forever at 1:24, the time of the explosion

tors turned off the turbogenerator trigger because it would have shut down the reactor as soon as the generators were turned off. This was the safety system that probably could have prevented the accident that was about to happen.

At 1:23:04 A.M., the steam that turned Turbogenerator Number Eight was blocked. Within 30 seconds, the turbine began to wind down, electric power dropped, water pumps slowed, the water supply to the core decreased, and more steam developed. More steam resulted in even less liquid water at the core, which resulted in higher reactivity. The higher reactivity produced more steam. As the system fed itself, heat production soared. At 1:23:40, operators, recognizing an emergency, hit the button that was to lower all control rods into the core and shut down the reactor.

It was probably too late to save the reactor. Ironically, however, this last attempt was the final straw. The reactor system had a design problem that no one had foreseen. The control rods had six-inch hollow tips at their lead ends. These tips enter the core before the boron carbide section. As they enter the core, they displace water. For a few seconds, they actually cause power to *increase*. Under normal operating conditions, this small and temporary increase has little effect.

But Chernobyl Reactor Number Four was not operating under normal conditions. As the control rod tips entered the core, power surged to 100 times normal in four seconds. Under intense heat, the core began to break down. Fuel assemblies fragmented, control rod channels warped, steam built up ferociously, and, finally, steam tubes burst. Tons of steam and water shot into the reactor, causing a tremendous steam explosion. The lid over the reactor, a 1,000-ton concrete disk ten feet thick, flipped into the air like a nickel and came back down to rest in an almost vertical position. Air rushed in, hit the white hot core and raging neutrons, and set off at least one chemical explosion.

Between the two (and possibly more) explosions, the roof over the reactor was destroyed. Hundreds of tons of nuclear fuel, graphite, and pieces of the reactor were hurled into the air. Most fell back into the reactor or within a radius of a few miles. Several tons of smaller particles, however, rose in a mile-high pillar of red heat to begin a deadly voyage around the world.

CHAPTER TWO
....

The Nature of Radiation

Atomic energy begins with an unstable atom, an isotope with too many or too few neutrons. To stabilize itself, the atom sheds neutrons and electrons, hurling them away at a regular rate, gradually breaking down into other isotopes. Uranium 235 is a naturally occurring radioactive isotope (or *radioisotope*). It is useful for nuclear fuel because when its neutrons collide with other U 235 atoms, they break up, releasing energy and more particles that go on to break up more atoms. The process, called fission, releases a lot of energy. Many of these new, smaller isotopes, such as strontium 90, strontium 89, tellurium 32, and iodine 131, are radioactive.

Sometimes the particles are absorbed by other atoms. When uranium 238 takes on an extra neutron, it becomes plutonium 239. Plutonium never existed until people set uranium into a chain reaction.

Like their forebears, these radioactive isotopes have a desperate need to balance themselves by shedding neutrons or electrons. As they do so, they emit energy. This energy, in the form of waves and subatomic particles, is the radioactivity that at high levels is so dangerous to living organisms.

Some isotopes very quickly throw off their destabilizing particles and thus return to a stable, natural state. Other isotopes take longer. Every eight days, half of a quantity of radioactive iodine 131 breaks down into xenon, an inert, nonradioactive element. These eight days are the *half-life* of that isotope. Every eight days, the quantity of the remaining radioactive iodine 131 is reduced by half. The half-life of strontium 90 is 28 years. The half-life of plutonium is 24,000 years. After ten half-lives, only 0.1 percent of the radioactivity remains so little it virtually disappears in the normal background radiation that exists around us. Iodine 131 takes 80 days to disappear. Plutonium 239 takes a quarter of a million years.

This decay process releases radiation. If radiation penetrates a cell and knocks an electron loose from a cell chemical, it forms an ion—a charged particle with an electrical need to form a new bond. Unfortunately, the new bond may not be one that nature intended for that cell. Fortunately, the body's immune system usually cleans up any damaged cells. Sometimes, however, the damage is to the cell's DNA, and if the immune system does not get rid of the cell, it can develop into cancer.

The radiation resulting from the accident at Chernobyl was of three varieties. One is an electromagnetic energy known as *gamma rays*. Like radio waves, microwaves, and waves of sunlight, gamma rays do not consist of particles. They are quite like X rays except that X rays are produced by an electrical device, while gamma rays are produced by atomic disintegration. Gamma rays can shoot through the human body and even penetrate a few feet of concrete.

Beta particles are electrons thrown off by decaying isotopes. Depending on their initial energy levels, they can travel 4 inches (8 to 10 centimeters) through the air and even penetrate up to an inch of human flesh. If they hit living tissue, they can damage cells. Beta particles are responsible for much of the skin injury that radiation victims suffer.

Alpha particles are the two neutrons and two protons that make up the nucleus of a helium atom. They are produced as heavy radioactive isotopes, such as uranium and plutonium, decay. Compared to beta particles, alpha particles are massive. Since they carry a strong positive electrical charge, they tend to react with the first thing they hit. If they hit the outside of a human body, they probably react with the thin layer of dead skin that surrounds the body and do no damage to the living tissue below. But if alpha particles get inside the body, their mass and charge make them 20 times more damaging than beta particles.

Measuring Radiation

Radiation is measured in various ways. The amount of radioactivity was originally measured in *curies*, named after Marie and Pierre Curie, who first isolated radium and polonium. One curie is that amount of material in which 37 billion atoms disintegrate per second. In the case of radium, the standard of measurement, one curie would be one gram. The accident at Three Mile Island is believed to have released 15 to 30 curies of harmful radionuclides into the atmosphere. Chernobyl may have released 500 million or more.

While curies are used to measure the quantity of radioactive material present in a given area, *roentgens* are used to measure the quantity of radiation present in the same area. Roentgens are measured using Geiger counters.

Curies and roentgens are helpful in determining how much radioactive material is present and how much radiation is being given off by that material, but neither indicate anything about how the radiation is affecting living tissue. The amount of radiation that is absorbed by living tissue is measured by the *rad*, which stands for *radiation absorbed dose*. A millirad is one-thousandth of a rad. A microrad is one-millionth of a rad.

Equal doses of different types of radiation do not produce the same biological damage. Gamma rays cause less damage; alpha particles inside the body cause more. To measure the biological effects of a dose of rads, scientists use the *rem*, which stands for *roentgen equivalent man*. The rem is a rad multiplied by a *quality factor*. The quality factor is determined by how effectively a particular radiation affects human tissue. The gamma ray is the standard. Its quality factor is one, so one rad of gamma radiation equals one rem. The rem for beta and alpha particles depends on whether they are inside or outside the body. Since alpha particles cannot penetrate skin, the rem is less than one if the particles are external. Inside the body, however, the rem is well above one.

Rems are only approximate measurements because the radiation is different for every isotope. The one rad emitted by strontium 90 is different from the one emitted by iodine 131. Their rem counts would be different. The problem is further complicated by the different ways each element's radiation affects living tissues.

The Effects of Radiation

Scientists have a hard time determining exactly how radiation affects the human body because humans are not guinea pigs. We cannot expose people to various types and levels of radiation to see how it affects them. The only way to see the effects of radiation is after individuals have been exposed under nonexperimental circumstances, such as after the atomic explosions at Hiroshima and Nagasaki, and nuclear accidents in laboratories and power plants.

Unfortunately, such incidents do not happen under the controlled conditions of a scientific experiment, and rarely are two individuals exposed in exactly the same way, and even when they are, other factors complicate the consequences. If, for example, three laboratory workers are exposed to a given source of radiation, it's possible that one might suffer cancer 20 years later while another dies of heart disease 30 years later, and the third suffers no apparent effects. Now suppose the first had a history of cancer in the family, the second smoked cigarettes, and the third drank lots of water. Suppose one was a young male, the other an older female, the third a younger female. Suppose one lived near a field often sprayed with pesticides, another lived near high-tension wires, and another used birth control pills.

With such inevitable differences in life-style, can the causes of their deaths be blamed on radiation? How do other factors—age, sex, life-style, and general health—contribute to ill effects years later? It's hard to say without performing parallel experiments on thousands of other people.

Just as humans are not guinea pigs, guinea pigs are not humans. Scientists can expose animals to various types and levels of radiation, but the effects are not the same as they would be on people. The results of exposing a mouse weighing x grams to y rads for z hours cannot be accurately converted to apply to a human of, say, 1000 (x) grams exposed to 1000 (y) rads for 1000 (z) hours. Furthermore, few animals live as long as humans, so long-term effects are hard to determine.

How much radiation is harmful to health? There is no simple answer to that question.

We are constantly bombarded by natural, or background, radiation. The sun and other cosmic sources expose the average American to 27 millirems per year. Rocks and soil add another 28 millirems. Radon seeping from the ground adds an average of 200 millirems. Medical X rays might add as much as 50 more. The human body itself is slightly radioactive. From these and other sources, the average American is exposed to about 360 millirems each year. This is nothing to worry about. It's been happening for as long as humans have lived on the earth. In general, our bodies are able to repair the minor damage done by these low levels of radiation.

A recent report, *The Biological Effects of Ionizing Radiation V* (*BEIR V*) attempted to determine whether there is a level of long-term radiation below which *no one* will suffer health problems. The report, the most thorough ever conducted on the issue, neither proved nor disproved the hypothesis that if the exposed population is large enough and exposed long enough, someone will suffer such ill effects as cancer and genetic mutation. Even normal background radiation, therefore, is responsible for a few cases of cancer. For this reason, doctors warn against letting basements fill with natural radon gas or exposing the skin to too much sunlight.

Some scientists claim that the cumulative effects of long-term low-dose radiation may be more harmful than single quick bursts of equal rems. Evidence for this is scanty, however, and some evidence seems to indicate the opposite. The *BEIR V* report could neither prove nor disprove the hypothesis.

At any rate, man-made radiation, from the X ray of a tooth to the explosion of atomic bombs, increases the level of radiation that hits us. The higher the level, the greater the number of people affected and the greater the number of diseases and deaths. But it must be noted that the number of lives *saved* by radiation—through X rays, nuclear medicine, and beneficial uses of radioactive materials—is millions of times greater than the deaths caused by the slight increase of background radiation in the environment or even the intense radiation resulting from nuclear accidents.

The U.S. federal government recommends that the general public be exposed to no more than 0.1 rem above natural background radiation levels in a year. People who work with radioactive materials or in radioactive environments may receive up to an average of 2 rems per year over the course of a few years.

These allowable levels have been dropping even lower. In 1934, it was thought that 30 rems was a healthy ceiling for occupational exposure. That maximum was cut to 15 rems in 1949, then to 5 rems in 1957, and then to 2 rems in 1990. Recommended public exposure dropped from 0.5 in 1956 to 0.17 in 1960 and to 0.1 in 1987.

Occupational exposure is allowed to be higher simply because fewer people are exposed. Statistically, the group of people exposed to these higher levels is so small that the total number of illnesses and deaths can be considered insignificant. The benefits of their work by far outweighs the risk that they, as a group, run.

What Radiation Does

Radiation can injure cells in two ways. High doses—generally those over 100 rems in a matter of hours—cause immediate and perceptible damage. Lower doses may simply start a cellular process that can take years or decades to produce illness.

Background radiation constantly bombards all living things on the earth. Since the levels are very low, the damage is very slight. In all but a very few cases, either the cells repair the damage done to them, or the immune system isolates and disposes of the injured cells.

The syndrome known as radiation sickness, which is caused by extremely high levels of radiation, goes through four phases. The prodromal phase occurs within minutes or hours. The victim feels an overwhelming nausea, fatigue, and vomiting. The effect is on the nervous system, not cell production.

Within a day or two, the victim enters the latent phase. Symptoms diminish or disappear. For two or three weeks, the victim seems to be recovering.

The severity of the next phase seems to depend on the level of dose. People receiving between 200 and 600 rads suffer a decrease in lymphocyte and white blood cells and platelets. Within a month, the victim suffers skin hemorrhage, ulcerated gums and nostrils, hair loss, diarrhea, fatigue, and chills. The immune system deteriorates. Normally minor infections from viruses and bacteria turn deadly. Victims exposed to more than

400 rads usually die within a month. Those who survive these first weeks may live for years but are likely to develop cancer.

People receiving 700 rads or more suffer the same initial injuries plus hemorrhaging and destruction of the intestinal lining. Blood vessels burst under the skin. After a brief period of latency, the victim suffers very high fever, delirium, dehydration, and failure of the circulatory system. Death follows within a week. The two Chernobyl victims who died within a week of the accident received doses higher than 700 rads.

The effects of lower doses are less obvious. They may take years to develop. Cancer is the most serious result. Apparently, radiation damages the DNA in cells. If the cells cannot repair this damage and they succeed in reproducing, the new cells have the same problem. Sometimes they grow out of control, building into a cancerous tumor.

When the DNA of reproductive cells is damaged, the result is often mutations and birth defects. Often the damage to human and animal fetuses is severe enough to cause spontaneous abortion. Those born live often suffer brain damage, Down's syndrome, below-average head size, and other abnormalities.

Other parts of the body are especially susceptible to damage from radiation. The lungs, thyroid, stomach, intestines, and bone marrow are most easily damaged. It is possible that one atom of plutonium—or at any rate a very minute amount of it—in the lung is enough to start cancerous growth. The thyroid, which tends to collect iodine, collects iodine 131 as well. The gland becomes a repository of radionuclides and a source of internal radiation for up to 80 days.

Strontium, being chemically similar to calcium, tends to attach itself to bones. There it remains, radiating into the marrow that produces the white blood cells that fend off disease. Under the constant bombardment of radiation, the marrow ceases to function the way it should. The result is often leukemia. A less obvious but very dangerous result is a breakdown in the body's immune system. Unable to defend itself from infection, the body readily contracts diseases and often fails to respond to medication.

Chernobyl offers doctors and scientists an unprecedented opportunity to study the effects of radiation on human life. Never before have so many people been exposed to so many different levels of radiation. Unfortunately, various factors are making accurate studies difficult. As explained later in this book, politics and money may be obscuring the truth about radiation and health. As time goes by, it becomes increasingly difficult to find and decipher clues and figure out what they mean to humanity.

CHAPTER THREE

....

The Liquidators

By 3:00 A.M. on April 26, Chernobyl director Bryukhanov informed his superiors in Moscow that there had been an explosion at Reactor Number Four. He gave them a relatively optimistic report. Radiation measurements, he said, showed levels within tolerable limits. This was true, in a certain sense, because the equipment they had was incapable of measuring levels any higher than those expected under normal conditions. The only adequate equipment was locked in a steel cabinet in the burning building.

Bryukhanov also reported that the reactor was intact. By his reasoning, it *had* to be intact because, as everyone knew, the reactor was perfectly safe. Bryukhanov reported that cooling water was being fed to the reactor. Apparently he believed this was true because the appropriate valve had been opened. When, at 9:00 A.M., an engineer climbed up to the roof of the building, peered in at the wreckage and reported what he saw—a white-hot glare in a pile of rubble and billowing smoke—Bryukhanov refused to believe it.

Chiefs, directors, and engineers from agencies involved in atomic energy boarded a jet to Kiev and from there took a helicopter to Chernobyl. By noon they were hovering 650 feet over the plant. Gazing into the gaping wound of pipes, girders, and rubble in the central hall, they saw the lid of the reactor, cherry red with heat, tilted up like the damper of a flue. Abandoned tangles of fire hose hung into the crater. A black circle of graphite lay a hundred yards (91 meters) around the plant. Though they had no radiometric equipment, it was clear they were looking at a very serious problem. They were also gaining a nice tan as the radiation seared their faces.

The cauldron below was brewing up every element and isotope in the periodic chart. As uncountable billions of neutrons shot around in chaos, they smashed into atoms, breaking them up and sending off more neutrons. Some isotopes existed for nanoseconds. Others boiled out into the sky to live for tens of thousands of years. Many of the elements and molecules, such as lead, are deadly for their chemical properties, let alone their radioactivity.

Communist party leaders in Pripyat reported the town still calm. Teams were practicing for the May Day games. Several weddings were taking place. Fearing panic more than radiation, the leaders began to discuss the pros and cons and possibilities of evacuation. A roadblock was set up to prevent anyone from entering or leaving the town.

Firemen, unaware that they were fighting an unquenchable atomic fire, assaulted the roof and aimed hoses into the flaming crater. They peered over the edge into the deadly abyss. Within seconds they absorbed enough radiation to kill them. They assumed that their violent nausea and overwhelming fatigue were caused by the smoke of burning chemicals. They assumed the toasted brown of their skin was from thermal heat.

The fire itself was no ordinary fire. At first, it was mostly burning tar on the roof. At some point, however, the thousand tons of graphite from the core ignited. Graphite is often used in industry because it withstands temperatures in excess of 4,500°F (2,500°C). Once it starts burning, however, it is very hard to extinguish. Water turns to steam before it reaches the flames. If there happens to be a white-hot core of melted nuclear fuel nearby, the steam decomposes into hydrogen and oxygen. As the hydrogen rises away from the heat, it ignites. In effect, the firemen were literally killing themselves to feed the fire.

The local defense militia was called in. Young soldiers were given gauze masks and cloth jumpsuits. An estimated 3,400 were assigned to clean nuclear fuel and graphite from the roof. They had no idea that they would be running through an environment of 10,000 to 20,000 rads per hour. They were allowed 90 seconds there, enough time to grab a chunk of something and toss it into the crater. After that minute-and-a-half shift, they could retire on a disability pension and take home a cash bonus to ease the consequences.

The world had never coped with such a disaster. No one had any idea what to do. The logical thing was to bury the fire and the tons of radionuclides that remained in the ruins of the reactor. The air force sent a fleet of helicopters. One by one they landed on the bank of the Pripyat River. Nuclear engineers, physicists and deputy ministers shoveled sand into bags as if doing penance in hell. Later they were helped by a hundred local farmers who had volunteered without knowing the kind of fire they were supposed to put out. Eventually someone thought of spreading out parachutes, filling them with sand, and having the helicopters lift them by their cords.

Helicopter pilots had to fly low so the sand bombs wouldn't stir up so much radioactive material or punch through the floor of the reactor. They also dropped loads of boron, to absorb neutrons; lead, to shield the radiation; and dolomite, which would break down into carbon dioxide and help smother the flames.

Two boys, evacuated from Chernobyl, hold a picture of their father, a fireman suffering from radiation poisoning.

A Soviet doctor involved in the cleanup of Chernobyl, himself suffering from radiation sickness, displays a picture of a helicopter dumping boron into the reactor.

The pilots and crews received radiation at a rate of several hundred rads per hour. Crew members had to lean out the doors into the upward flood of radionuclides to see when to release the loads. In a single flight they would take in several years of allowable dosage. They flew until they were too weak and nauseated to hold the controls of their helicopters.

There was fear that the collapsing rubble of nuclear fuel would become too concentrated. If it did, it could reach critical mass and set off a true atomic explosion, destroying the neighboring three reactors. Reactors One, Two, and Three were shut down. Reactor Three was in immediate danger of burning, so its nuclear fuel had to be carried to safe areas some distance away. Workers piled lead capsules of nuclear fuel on platforms with handles and ran just as fast as their legs could carry them.

The First Victims

Number Six Clinic in Moscow didn't quite know what to do with the sudden influx of radioactive patients. The first bunch had to wait outside. Still dressed in the summer clothes they'd been wearing in Ukraine, they shivered in the cold Moscow air while patients with more normal ailments were admitted ahead of them. The delay was to allow staff to set up equipment that had been stored in case of nuclear war. The doctors who finally came to escort them were wearing protective gear. They installed each patient in a bed under a plastic tent and examined wounds by reaching through holes in the tent.

No other patients shared that floor of the hospital. Later, when radiation was detected on floors above and below the Chernobyl victims, other patients were moved still farther away. Doctors requested extra pay for working under hazardous conditions.

The victims suffered from radiation and heat burns. Their skin was browned like toasted marshmallow. In some places it was black like burned marshmallow. Their skin cracked, blistered, peeled, hung in strips. The slightest movement could cause it to tear open. The wounds did not heal. Their hair fell out. Muscles separated from bones like overcooked meat. Iodine 131 had collected in their thyroids. Strontium 90 had collected in their bones. Cesium and plutonium had spread through their bodies.

The patients themselves were toxic waste. Victims who arrived later and lay in those beds became more radioactive than they had been when they arrived.

Boris Stolyarchuk, the senior control engineer on duty at the time of the explosion, was among the first victims taken to Number Six Clinic. He was still alive in 1992, though suffering from cardiovascular and digestive tract problems. He reports that he has gotten more attention from KGB agents than from doctors. The agents started in Pripyat and continued at Number Six Clinic, sending agent after agent to hear his testimony again and again. The interrogations continued while he was shaking from fear and vomiting uncontrollably. He saw himself possibly dying of radiation poisoning, and possibly being imprisoned for blowing up a nuclear power plant. He wasn't sure which fate he preferred.

For a week he wasn't sure whether he had caused the accident. He told the agents exactly what he did and what he remembered happening. He told them he had followed his instructions perfectly.

And indeed he had. That, says Stolyarchuk, was the source of his fear. The detailed plan for the test of Turbogenerator Number Eight had virtually doomed the reactor. The responsible authorities, he says now, were hoping to blame the disaster on human error somewhere below them. But he couldn't say that to the KGB, which was forcing him to walk the terrifying edge between accused criminal and witness for the prosecution.

As Stolyarchuk lay in bed in Number Six Clinic, he kept asking what had become of his colleagues. One, he knew, was still inside the Chernobyl plant, his body surrounded by radiation that would kill anyone who went near. He had run to open a water valve near the core, a desperate attempt to cool a reactor that no longer existed.

No one would answer Stolyarchuk's questions. The fate of his colleagues was none of his business, they said. His business was to tell them the truth about what happened just before the explosion. The truth they wanted, of course, was their version of the truth, not his.

The guards in the hall and the women who washed radiation from the floors had news. They could be bribed with cigarettes. They reported death after death. In the first few weeks, 26 people died. Six were firemen, 20 were engineers and operators at the plant. Their radioactive bodies were taken to a cemetery called Mitino, just outside of Moscow. Boris Stolyarchuk knew most of the dead and assumed he would soon join them.

Mitino was a new cemetery. In the next few years it would be used exclusively for thousands of liquidators—those who helped clean up the radioactive mess. They were given their own cemetery to isolate their strontium-infected bones from the rest of the world. The first victims, the firemen, are buried in lead-lined coffins soldered shut, preventing their radioactive remains from joining the dust of the earth. The size of the Mitino cemetery is one of few clues to the number of deaths caused by the accident at Chernobyl. While the Soviet government denied more than 254 deaths, the cemetery kept growing.

Stolyarchuk's health wavered for the next two months. He was transferred to a sanitarium outside Leningrad. His explanations held up through repeated interrogations. When he was released in Kiev, he was given 50 rubles—worth just a few dollars—and two nights in a hotel. Then he had to go find himself some clothes and a place to live. Everything he owned was back in Pripyat, untouchable for the next several centuries. He stayed with friends for several months until the government gave him a room in a boardinghouse. Later, he married another liquidator. They had a daughter. To their relief, she was born normal, though like most children in Kiev she is often sick with ailments doctors can't quite identify. In 1991 he finally received a letter from the Soviet government. It said the accident wasn't his fault.

Dousing the Atomic Fire

By May 1 the pile of sand, boron, and lead seemed to have done the trick. The flames died. Smoke dwindled to a wisp. Radioactive emissions subsided. Though still watching clouds of radionuclides settle over Europe and rise into the jet stream, the world felt relieved to see the disaster diminish after only four days. The Soviet Union reported only two dead and 197 hospitalized. It seemed the disaster wasn't nearly as bad as it might have been.

But on May 3 the level of radioactive emission started rising again. Firemen discovered they were dealing with a kind of fire that doesn't go out when smothered. It just gets worse. The burial of the core only trapped the heat, which caused an increase in reactivity. Internal temperatures shot up to over 3,600°F (2,000°C). There was talk of the possibility of the concentrated nuclear materials reaching critical mass and exploding like an atomic bomb.

A more probable event was the melting of the floor beneath the reactor. This was all the more likely because of the 4,000 tons of materials that had been thrown on top of the core. If the whole white-hot mess fell into the suppression pool below the reactor, the water there would instantly vaporize and explode, throwing the remainder of the fuel and tons of radioactive steam into the atmosphere.

No one had ever made plans for such a situation. No one knew with certainty what to do. Except for nuclear war, this was probably the biggest emergency mankind could possibly devise. Solutions, however, had to be dreamed up on the spot, under pressure and without possibility of experiment.

The best solution seemed to be to first drain the water from the suppression pool, then inject liquid nitrogen around the bottom of the core. The nitrogen would cool the core, lower reactivity, and replace the air that could cause a flare-up. To drain the suppression pool, however, workers had to enter the reactor building, climb through radioactive rubble, find the drain valve, and open it. The workers who did so almost certainly absorbed a deadly dose of radiation. As with most of the 600,000 liquidators, information on their fate is not available.

To feed in the nitrogen was even more dangerous. To open a way for a pipeline, military workers shot armor-piercing shells at the wall. The hole was too small, however. Next they blasted a hole in the wall, but they found that rubble of concrete, broken pipe, and other materials blocked the way. The next best plan was to send welders into the building to cut a hole through a certain corridor wall. A team of courageous workers went in and did the job, but it probably cost them their lives.

The Sarcophagus

The fire was not considered out until May 6. It had taken ten days, and the situation was still far from under control. It could only be said that it wasn't getting worse. The release of radiation had slowed considerably, but by pre-Chernobyl standards it was still disastrously high. Until the end of May, the daily release was more than the total release at Three Mile Island. Leakage would continue until October.

The next stage of recovery was to build a "sarcophagus" around the radioactive ruins and clean up some of the radioactive mess that lay around it. The Soviets hoped to use robotic bulldozers to do some of this. Even before the fire was out, remote-control machines were set on the roof, but they turned out to be useless. One got tangled up in the fire hoses. Another lost its electronic circuitry to the barrage of radiation. In the end, humans had to clean up the mess they'd made. People called the workers "biological robots."

No protective gear was efficient enough to withstand the high levels of radiation. Most workers were given only cloth jumpsuits, rubber boots, and respirators that filtered out only a little of the radioactive dust. Bulldozers were equipped with lead cabins, and buses to the site had lead plates hung over the windows. Many of the workers had no idea what danger they faced. They saw no threat and felt no pain. They were quite content to be receiving double salaries and extra rations of vodka, which supposedly would make their bodies less susceptible to radiation. The job was gargantuan. A structure of steel plates had to be welded over the entire building. More than 14 million cubic feet (400,000 cubic meters) of concrete had to be mixed at the site and poured into

Technicians and liquidators inside the sarcophagus

concrete barriers that were moved into place by bulldozers. New pavement had to be laid down all around the plant. Miners, many of them workers who had built the subway system in Kiev, were all but forced to tunnel under the plant to build concrete supports beneath the core. They also had to build a wall 45 feet (17.5 meters) into the ground to prevent contaminated rainwater from mixing with groundwater. All this work was done under radioactive conditions far in excess of those allowed by law.

Helicopters sprayed a plastic film over exposed soil to catch and hold radionuclides. Eventually, bulldozers scraped up several inches of topsoil from hundreds of acres. Other farmland was simply plowed under to put the radionuclides beneath a few inches of soil. Dikes had to be built to keep rainwater from washing radionuclides into the Pripyat River and from there to the Dnieper, which flowed through Kiev and into the Black Sea. Abandoned pets in Pripyat, many of which were soon blind and too weak to walk, had to be hunted down, shot, and buried along with contaminated cars, tools and wastes.

Contaminated farm animals were rounded up and moved from the area. While they were fattened up for slaughter, their manure was radioactive enough to be treated as hazardous waste. To dilute the exposure of people who consumed the 10,000 tons of meat from these animals, much of it was ground up and mixed with uncontaminated meat at a ratio of one to ten. Many workers in meat-packing plants reported feeling ill when working with the meat. Some undiluted meat was shipped to the far corners of the Soviet Union so that no one individual would eat enough to accumulate a dangerous dose. Secret government documents made public in 1991 revealed that 47.5 tons of meat and 2 million tons of milk were produced in contaminated areas.

Since trees and other plants tend to suck up radioactive water and hold the isotopes in their cells, and since radioactive dust tends to settle on leaves, vast areas of forest were completely leveled. Since burning the wood would have sent the isotopes back into the atmosphere, the wood had to be buried. As far away as Kiev, leaves fallen from trees had to be raked up and buried. Citizens remember schoolchildren being ordered to gather the radioactive leaves in their arms and carry them into trucks.

In all, over 600,000 liquidators worked on the cleanup. This number includes anyone who entered the "Prohibited Zone" that reaches 18 miles (30 kilometers) around the plant. It is estimated that about 200,000 received high doses. Years later the government offered liquidators special health and retirement benefits, not to mention an official medal featuring a drop of blood and symbols for alpha, beta, and gamma. But many liquidators complain that the men who were sent on suicide missions onto the roof or into the building were receiving the same benefits as those who merely drove a bus into fringes of the Zone.

During the cleanup, civilian workers were expected to stay at the site for 12 hours, then spend 12 hours away. They were not supposed to receive more than the allowable lifetime dose of 35 rads. Doctors, however, have unofficially reported many people arriving in clinics after exposure to 200 rads or more. Only a few workers wore personal dosimeter badges, and these could be read only at a special laboratory. Workers turned in their badges only after a day's work, by which time they may have received more than the allowable lifetime dose. Official records tend to show great numbers with the maximum allowed dose—no more, no less.

Soldiers, many from the military reserve, suffered even greater exposure. Some stayed in the Zone through the summer and into November. They slept in tents a few miles from the site, exposed to the radioactive breeze. Most worked with no protective clothing and had no shower facilities where they could wash the radionuclides from their bodies. Without protective clothing or respirators, they patrolled within a few yards of the reactor. No one explained the danger they were in.

No one knows what became of many of those 600,000 liquidators. Most of the soldiers were later transferred to points throughout the Soviet Union. If any collective records were kept of their fate, they are still secret. No complete records are available on civilian liquidators. The Ukrainian Ministry of Health says it has a registry of 129,000 liquidators, including dose estimates for 56,000 people who received 10 to 20 rems. The Soviet government claimed to have records for 37,500 liquidators hospitalized between 1986 and 1988. The accuracy and quality of dose and medical estimations, however, are suspected to be inadequate, and there has been little cooperation between Soviet and Ukrainian agencies. No statistical information on liquidators as a whole is available to the public.

Only in 1991 did liquidators begin to seek one another out in the hope of finding something closer to the truth. Liquidators in Ukraine formed an association, called The Chernobyl Union. For the first time they, not a government, began collecting statistics about how many liquidators have died of cancer, brain hemorrhage, blood disease, and other diseases possibly related to exposure to radiation.

As the Soviet Union broke up into several independent states in late 1991, it became all the more difficult to gather information.

So far various individuals and organizations are only estimating how many have died. Estimates range from 3,000 to 10,000, though officials in Moscow were still claiming the number of deaths is under 300, and the former Ukrainian minister of health, Anatoly Romanenko, who became director of the Ukrainian Institute of Radiology, still maintained that the only health problem was stress and that the only cure was to stop worrying about it.

CHAPTER FOUR

....

An Unhealthy Environment

T he biggest and most important controversy in the wake
of the Chernobyl disaster concerns long-term health. How has
radiation affected the health of people who lived nearby, or hundreds of miles away, or on the other side of the world? The
answers, muddled by conflicting motivations, may never be
known.

The number of estimated deaths ranges between incredible
extremes. As of the end of 1991, the Soviet government in Moscow
admitted to 254 deaths due to acute radiation sickness (ARS). The
Chernobyl Union claims that as many as 10,000 workers have
already died from a number of illnesses. Statistics of death rates
in the United States indicate the possibility of thousands of additional deaths in the months following the accident. Some cancer
specialists are predicting an eventual total of several million cancer cases and as many as half a million deaths from cancer
throughout Europe, Asia, and the Middle East. Other specialists
say the worldwide increase will be under 1,000 over the next 50
years—a total far below that caused by medical X rays or radon.

Just as uncertain are the less dreadful effects of Chernobyl's
radiation on the human body. Acute radiation sickness is easy to

diagnose and hard to deny. Other possible effects, however, are harder to link to a specific cause. In contaminated areas in Ukraine, Belarus, and Russia, Chernobyl is being blamed for everything from cancer and birth defects to bloody noses and sore throats. These and other illnesses that may be caused by radiation may also be caused by other factors. Malnutrition, exposure to chemical pollution, and mental stress can lead to similar ill effects.

The confusion and controversy is a product of conflicting fears, purposes, and unknown factors. Science, having never studied such a situation, doesn't even claim to have the definite answers. Politicians, more certain of themselves, either want to minimize or exaggerate the truth, depending, apparently, on their personal motivations. The atomic energy industry is being accused of hiding or distorting the truth. Bureaucrats may be

Soviet health officials take information from people reporting health problems after the Chernobyl disaster.

burying or even destroying information to protect themselves from blame. Mothers of sick children are either perceiving what scientists cannot observe or are making accusations in blind and desperate hysteria. Doctors are frustrated by the lack of reliable statistics as well as by the lack of reliable tools for diagnoses. Together, this mix of motives and lack of data produces results that are more confusing than conclusive.

Information Deficiency

It is often impossible to link cancer to a specific cause. The tumor that starts to grow in a middle-aged adult could have been caused by contact with a carcinogen during childhood. Since virtually every human being comes into contact with some amount of cigarette smoke, pesticides, fertilizers, steroids, X rays, natural and man-made radiation, lead vapors, food additives, and other suspected carcinogens, it is hard to determine what specifically has caused people to develop cancer.

To discover the probable causes of cancer, oncologists need to use statistical information. To establish the link between cigarettes and lung cancer, for example, they analyzed life-style data from thousands of lung cancer victims. They then compared the data with that of control groups with similar habits and life-styles but no traces of cancer. While the cancer group and control group had similar rates of exposure to other possible causes, the cancer group had a higher rate of cigarette use.

For this kind of research, scientists need a lot of accurate and carefully selected information. Unfortunately, such information is very scarce in the former Soviet republics. Before *glasnost*, Soviet people had virtually no freedom to record and exchange information. The Soviet government had the power to tell doctors and scientists how to record health data. Even before the Chernobyl incident, information was falsely recorded or later manipulated to hide health problems. Cancer rates were already high because of radiation and chemical pollution. Soviet statistics, however, showed a relatively low cancer rate.

Immediately after the Chernobyl incident, despite the new policy of glasnost, doctors were ordered not to diagnose or record any illness as a possible consequence of radiation. If they did so, they could lose their jobs and even go to prison. Children with thyroid problems were listed as having strep throat. Pneumonia was diagnosed as bronchitis.

Statistics are further confused by special medical efforts made after the accident. After 1988 all people in areas affected by Chernobyl were required to see a doctor once a year. With more people seeing doctors more often, more health problems were detected. The apparent increase in disease, therefore, is, to some indeterminable extent, only an increase in the *detection* of disease.

No statistical records—at least none available to the public— were kept for liquidators. Those in the army were often transferred to other areas of the Soviet Union, effectively disappearing. Their whereabouts and current state of health are not known. The medical records of some 67,000 radiation exposures in Ukraine were apparently stolen and destroyed. Many of the extant records were most certainly falsified. Since regulations prohibited any individual from receiving more than 35 rads, most records show no more than that. Many of the helicopter pilots and firemen, however, certainly received hundreds of rads.

Meanwhile, the Soviet Union has ceased to exist. The new national governments, especially those of Ukraine and Belarus, are very interested in determining how their populations are suffering from radiation. Unfortunately, the Russian government, apparently hoping to avoid responsibility for the accident and the expense of compensating victims, may not be offering as much information, or as accurate information, as it has. It is impossible to say, with any clinical accuracy, how much the incidence of cancer, asthma, pneumonia, tuberculosis, diphtheria, birth defects, anemia, cardiovascular disease, immune deficiency, and gastrointestinal problems has increased. Doctors have no doubt, however, that all of these diseases are much more common than in the past.

The Forecast: Worsening Health

The effects of long-term low-dose radiation take years to develop. To predict increases in cancer and other health problems, scientists have been using data collected from Hiroshima and Nagasaki, the only prior incidents that involved thousands of people. The experience of atomic bomb survivors from those cities indicates that cancer rates will rise, though not much above normal levels. Increases in leukemia and thyroid cancer in those cities came only after about ten years.

The effects of those two atomic bombings, however, are likely to be quite different from those of Chernobyl. The source, type, and amount of radiation were different. (The Hiroshima bomb used only 4.5 tons of fuel, while Chernobyl released 50 tons.) Since the bombings happened during a war, the population was predominantly women, elderly people, and very young children.

Food came into the city from nonradioactive sources. Also, those who survived the initial bombing, fire, and widespread disease tended to be of stronger constitution than the average population and therefore were less likely to die of cancer in later years.

So far, it looks like the populations around Chernobyl are going to suffer long-term problems far worse than those in Hiroshima and Nagasaki. The cancer cases expected ten years in the future were developing just five years after the accident. A Ukrainian epidemiologist working in Belarus found cancer had increased 45 percent between 1985 and 1990 in "dirty" areas, but only 11 percent in less radioactive areas. By 1991, cases of thyroid cancer in children were increasing very quickly. This ailment was virtually unknown before Chernobyl. Doctors do not remember diagnosing more than one case per year in a given region. By 1991, there were 38 cases in the heavily contaminated Gomel region of Belarus, and 131 in six regions around Minsk, the capital of Belarus. Incidence of goiters (a non-cancerous enlargement of the thyroid) in "dirty" areas of Belarus increased 1,500 percent but merely doubled in cleaner (though by no means uncontaminated) areas. Scientists from the World Health Organization (WHO) confirmed the data.

A similar situation was developing in Ukraine. In 1983, there were 3 cases of thyroid cancer. In 1984, just 1. There were 2 per year from 1985 to 1987. In 1989, however, there were 6, and in 1990, 21. All of them had lived in Zone One, the most contaminated area. Some were still fetuses when Chernobyl exploded.

Still, doctors are hesitant to claim a scientific link between Chernobyl's iodine 131 and the cases of cancer. To firmly establish the connection, they need to know how much iodine 131 the average child, and the patients, received or when or whether they were given doses of iodine to fill the thyroid before radioactive iodine could enter. Since iodine 131 has such a short half-life, it had to be measured within 80 days of exposure. (In cases where it was measured immediately after the accident, some children's thyroids were emitting 300 millirads per hour—more than the annual dose allowed in the United States.) By the time cancer and other thyroid problems develop, the possible cause has disappeared.

Increases in other forms of cancer began to appear in the early 1990s, a few years sooner than expected. Again, data is scattered and not readily attributed to radiation. In a Belarusan town 50 miles north of Chernobyl, the frequency of malignant tumors increased from 210 cases per 100,000 people in 1986 to 337 cases in 1990.

At the Children's Hematology Center in Minsk, doctors report a doubling of leukemia rates since 1986, though the rates before that cannot be confirmed. Some of the increase may be the result of increased monitoring of public health. In Ukraine, leukemia rates were stable in the 1980s but seemed to be increasing slightly in the early 1990s. Doctors still lacked statistical evidence of increased rates but expected to see more cases after 1993.

Leonid V. Skripka, an elected representative in the municipal government of Kiev, a former plant biologist, gathered information from several hospitals in Kiev and also from the Academy of Science where he once worked. Some of his information came from the KGB, the Soviet Union's secretive information agency, which was dissolved in Ukraine when the republic won its independence. He said official records listed 30,000 victims of Chernobyl, but there were probably another 20,000 who hadn't bothered to register.

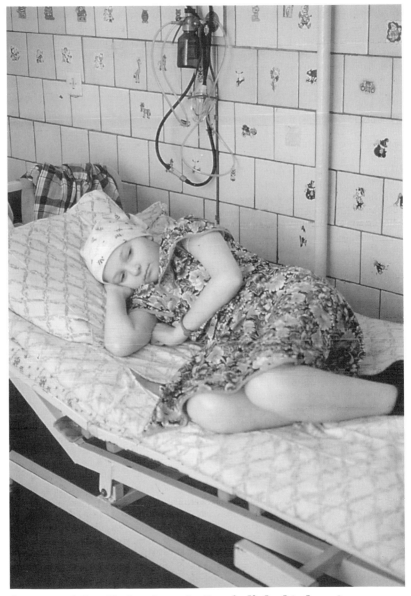

**A young girl suffering from leukemia linked to long-term
exposure to low-level radiation**

Personally, however, Skripka considers all 2.6 million people in Kiev to be victims because radiation levels were and still are higher than officially recognized. Secret KGB data indicated radioactive elements in virtually all residents. Shortly after the accident, one-year-old children had an average of .5 rem of iodine in their thyroids. Pregnant women were found to have radioactive particles in their blood. Nursing mothers had it in their milk. Blood donor data in 1990 showed that 80 percent of the population had abnormal blood, especially in immunological proteins. Because of this, 30 percent of children in Kiev could not receive a vaccine without contracting the very disease the vaccine was meant to prevent.

According to Skripka's data, the death rate among officially registered victims of Chernobyl rose 400 percent from 1987 to 1991. Cancer rates were up 300 percent and expected to climb sharply. Half of the deaths from gastrointestinal cancers were from internal radiation. Breast cancer was up 26 percent but could not be linked to radiation because there was no way to measure how much radiation the women had consumed. Generally, cases of all disease had increased 500 percent. Respiratory disease, not including cancer and tuberculosis, was up 2,000 percent. Pneumonia rose 220 percent in adults and 260 percent in children. Cancer of the brain rose 350 percent. Genetic aberrations in heavily contaminated areas (not Kiev) had risen over 1,000 percent.

Experiments with animals—mostly white rats—are producing no good news for the future. Rats receiving food with low doses of radiation tend to develop cancer within nine months, while those receiving clean food develop cancer much less often and only after 16 months. Scientists are not sure how to evaluate the data, however, because the rats received very carefully balanced diets, while people in Belarus, Russia, and Ukraine do not.

The director of the Kiev morgue says that he was never asked to try to link radiation to patterns in causes of death. Shortly after the accident, a few specific cadavers were identified as those of liquidators, and the morgue was directed to remove certain organs and send them to the Institute of Pharmacology and Toxicology. He was never told why or what was learned from any tests that were done.

In subsequent years, morgue personnel detected two startling facts. The "sudden death" rate—that is, death occurring to people not under the care of a doctor—among relatively young adults had increased from about 4,000 per year in 1987 to about 6,000 in 1991. Heart diseases, including heart attacks and blood diseases, were the biggest killer. (The same is true of heart disease in the general population of the United States.) There is no single explanation for these deaths, though Chernobyl seems a likely culprit.

The morgue director suspected that alcoholism was also a significant factor. Many liquidators drank too much because they were on disability and had nothing else to do. Others drank in the erroneous hope that it would alleviate the effects of radiation. Others drank in despair over their health and the general future of their country. Also, many of the deaths may have fallen into the "sudden" category because of various reasons people did not go to doctors: no effective care, fear of hearing their illness was terminal, or resignation that radiation would make an early death inevitable.

The second startling fact that the director noticed was a soaring rate of brain hemorrhage among men under the age of 30.

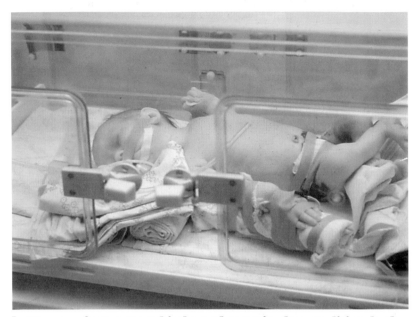

Instances of premature births and genetic abnormalities, both linked to radiation exposure, have risen dramatically since the Chernobyl explosion.

This had virtually never happened before Chernobyl. Now it was common. Thinner blood vessels—a known result of exposure to radiation, though also of malnutrition and alcoholism—was the immediate cause of hemorrhage.

Meanwhile, at the other end of the range of human life, a hospital in Kiev reported that only half of babies were born without health problems. The birth rate had declined dramatically, but the number of premature babies was remaining constant. As of 1991, the number of birth defects among babies born of mothers not from highly contaminated areas, however, had not risen. The biggest problem, said doctors, was a lack of supplies and equipment. Disposable diapers were not available. There was no equipment to warm premature babies, measure blood pressure, or regulate intravenous solutions. Hypodermic needles were used so often they had to be resharpened. Infections were especially high because adult patients were interned nearby.

Overall, the rate of death in Ukraine now exceeds the rate of birth by about 40,000 per year. A biologist in Kiev summed up the situation rather succinctly. She said that Ukrainians could be considered an endangered species. If the current trend continued long enough, they would become extinct.

Chernobyl AIDS

Virtually every doctor in Ukraine and Belarus has noticed a strange thing happening in public health. Simply put, people are getting sick more often, and their sicknesses are worse than they used to be. Allergies are more common and more serious. Pregnant women experience more complications and suffer them earlier in the pregnancy, and more women die during childbirth. Pulmonary problems, from asthma to cancer, have increased tremendously. Simple illnesses such as colds and flu are worse and last longer. Surgical operations are riskier and more difficult because the body has trouble recovering from surgical wounds and minor infections. People report vague dizziness and temporary blackouts and loss of consciousness.

The problem is affecting children most of all. Only 35 percent of schoolchildren in Kiev are free of health problems. Twenty-five percent of children evacuated from Pripyat have weakened heart muscles. Such common childhood diseases as measles and chicken pox take much longer to cure. Nosebleeds are far more common than in the past. Minor wounds take longer to heal. Stomachaches are almost constant. Children come home from school so fatigued they can hardly walk.

A most disturbing fact is that people's bodies do not respond to medication as they should. A medicine meant to lower blood pressure, for example, might touch off a fever. Medication meant to reduce anemia might increase it. Complex diseases such as leukemia are extremely difficult to treat.

One doctor at a pediatric hospital expressed the problem well. He said that every case of illness, and its treatment, is unique. Measles in one child is different from that in another. The information in textbooks is not valid. The treatments developed after years of experiments with laboratory animals are no longer valid. Doctors must practice what they call "catastrophe medicine," offering untried treatments and waiting to see how the patient responds. In effect, the patient is an experimental animal, though without the benefits that such animals normally receive: a sterile environment, a balanced diet, and uncontaminated food, water, and air.

The doctors are calling the problem "Chernobyl AIDS." It is, literally, an acute immune deficiency syndrome, though it is not related to HIV and is not contagious. Though doctors are scientifically hesitant to blame radiation for every case of cancer and genetic abnormality, they are virtually unanimous in concluding that radiation is the cause of the syndrome.

Radiation is known to damage the immune system. Strontium attached to the bones radiates into the marrow that produces white blood cells. Plutonium and cesium tend to spread throughout the body. Though less concentrated than the iodine 131 that collects in the thyroid, these isotopes remain active for the lifetime of an individual. Their radiation attacks, among other things, the lymphocyte system that fights off infections.

Holistic Illness

Radiation is by no means the only factor contributing to poor health in the regions affected by Chernobyl. The Soviet territory is an environmental nightmare. In the Communist effort to maintain production, environmental safeguards were ignored. Dangerous nitrate-rich fertilizers were used, as were pesticides that have been banned in many other countries. Gasoline still contains lead, and cars have no pollution-control devices. Non atomic power plants spew untreated exhaust into the air. Factories dump toxic waste into rivers.

Malnutrition weakens the body's defenses against this environmental onslaught. The peoples of the Soviet Union never had a very rich or varied diet. With radioactive contamination of soil making much of Ukraine and Belarus unsafe for agriculture, the situation has grown more dire. And whether or not food is actually contaminated, people tend to believe it is. When a mother has the good fortune to find milk for her children, she has to wonder if it contains radioactive strontium. With a large portion of the population avoiding milk, they suffer deficiencies in calcium, an element essential to the immune system.

Cigarette smoke and alcohol are also major factors. Although Mikhail Gorbachev instituted some restrictions on alcohol consumption, many people still produce vodka in homemade stills. A majority of adults smoke cigarettes, and those who don't, including children, are subjected to daily doses of second-hand smoke.

On top of this, everyone is under the kind of stress that can lead to health problems, especially heart disease. People are unsure about their new political independence. Civil unrest threatens to build into civil war. People fear an early death from cancer or heart disease brought on by radiation. They are advised not to swim in rivers because radiation tends to flow into them, not to walk in forests because radiation lingers in soil and becomes concentrated in plants, and not to lie in the natural cosmic radiation of the sun. They suspect that future generations will suffer these same problems plus an increasing number of birth defects. With national economies all but comatose and inflation out of control, they expect chronic unemployment and general shortages of everything from food and clothing to electricity and health care. Financial problems lead to family problems, which in turn add to stress.

All of these factors—pollution, malnutrition, stress—add up to more than whatever their total individual effects might be. Doctors call this phenomenon *synergy*. Synergy figures into the complexity of the health situation. Not only are symptoms and responses to medicine more complex, but their possible causes are complex, too. The attacks of chemical and radiological pollution, malnutrition, and stress tend to help one another weaken the body's defense.

One Ukrainian doctor said the problem might better be seen as an unprecedented opportunity for advances in medicine. With such a huge population of patients, researchers should be able to learn a lot about how the human body reacts to a polluted environment. They can also learn about the immune system, perhaps even find clues to a cure for HIV/AIDS. He felt that the solution to the Chernobyl situation is not more doctors and hospitals but rather the development of a new medical specialty to deal with "holistic illness"–the general breakdown of health.

Such a specialty is already taking shape in Kiev. One hospital has developed special computer software to deal with the complex problems caused by "Chernobyl AIDS." The program ana-

A mother in Pripyat holds the handwritten record of her child's health problems since Chernobyl.

lyzes all of a body's functions and devises a holistic treatment for the whole body, not just a single symptom. Ironically, the hospital was unable to use the software because it had no ribbons for the computer printer.

Counting The Deaths

It is simply impossible to realistically estimate how many people have died and will die as a result of exposure to Chernobyl's radiation. The lowest estimates are 200 to 600 deaths, all in the region of the former Soviet Union. The highest is 500,000 throughout the world. The real toll, however, could be much higher if indirect deaths are included. Acute radiation sickness represents only the tiniest fraction of the total. Even the predicted number of cases of cancer is small compared to the bigger, vaguer picture. Tens of thousands of people have died or will die from diseases they might have survived if their immune systems were normal. More thousands will die because of fear of vaccinations. The increase of disease in radiation victims will likely increase disease among others.

The contamination of the best farmland in the region has aggravated an already serious problem with malnourishment. As if that weren't enough, fear of contaminated food, especially milk, greens, and meat, leaves people deficient in the vitamins they need to stay healthy. The health problem is not actual starvation but rather a weakness in the face of other deadly health problems.

Many people will suffer, and perhaps die, because of medical care that has been shifted to care for Chernobyl victims. Many others receive inadequate care because doctors are afraid to live in contaminated areas. Many will die because their bodies cannot tolerate surgical operations. Many die before they are born. It is estimated that hundreds of thousands of pregnant women had abortions—some very late in the pregnancy—just after the accident; in some cases, the women died, too.

The final death toll, therefore, will never be known. To deny that these indirect and often long-delayed deaths were the result of the accident at Chernobyl would be to deny reality. Considering that several tons of nuclear fuel still sit in the sarcophagus, and that several more tons of radionuclides will be blowing around the world for the next several centuries, the official total of 254 is a cruel distortion of the truth. An estimate in the tens of thousands would not be unrealistic, and eventual death tolls in the hundreds of thousands may be possible.

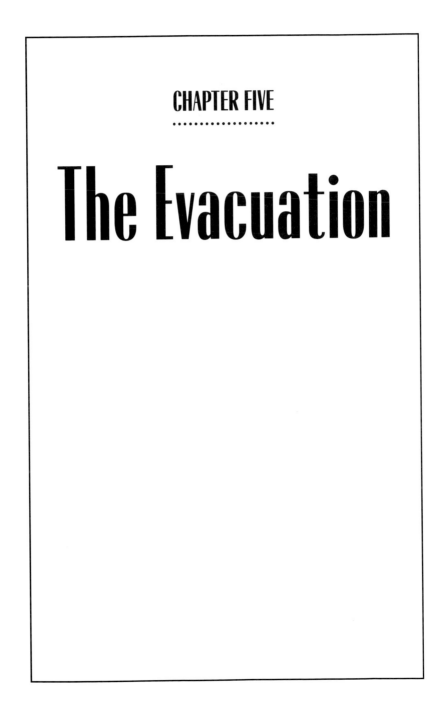

CHAPTER FIVE

The Evacuation

April 26 was a Saturday. During the night, the first warm breezes of spring were blowing across Ukraine. For the first time since the summer before, Valentina Patushina and 40,000 other people in Pripyat slept with their windows open. Late that night an explosion jolted her awake. A few seconds later she heard another. It sounded like a car backfiring. Who, she wondered, was trying to start a car at 1:24 in the morning? She considered closing the windows, but the explosions stopped, and the breeze felt so nice. She went back to sleep. It never occurred to her that it was a nuclear power plant backfiring, that the breeze was deadly, and that closing the windows would be a very good idea.

When the sun came up, Valentina noticed a peculiar slimy foam in the streets. It was like the detergent foam the street-cleaning machines sometimes left, except the bubbles didn't pop and settle down. It was ankle deep for several hours.

She called a friend, Natasha, who lived at the edge of town that faced the power plant. Natasha said she could see black smoke clouding the power plant. Was there some connection between the smoke and the foam? Natasha *felt* some connection. But Valentina, a biologist and teacher, said no, the power plant was safe. There might be a fire, but it was simply impossible for anything to endanger the town. The reactor had several levels of safety protection. A serious accident was impossible. Everybody knew that. So Valentina and all the other mothers in town sent their children to school. They had to go. The May 1 Labor Day celebrations were coming up. Everyone had to prepare. The children set out into the springtime in short pants and short sleeves, wading through the foam. Valentina, being a teacher, went, too.

At school, the administration made a special announcement. Doctors were coming to dispense special Iodine pills. Each child would get one. No one was allowed outdoors. But there was nothing to be concerned about. Preparations for the May Day games should proceed.

By noon, spring fever reached an uncontrollable pitch. Kids were leaking out of the school like bees from a hive. It was time to go home. Teachers, following orders, told them to go straight home but to stay indoors. There was no explanation of how they should go home without going outside. It made little sense, so it didn't seem to matter. Besides, nothing seemed amiss. It was the kind of day when you're *supposed* to play outdoors. It was *good* for you.

So that's just what the kids did. They played in grass laced with plutonium. They played in sand mixed with radioactive graphite. They jumped in the piles of radioactive foam and raced through the radioactive breeze. They picked radioactive flowers and stuck them in their radioactive hair. They saw radioactive helicopters landing in open lots and ran up to touch them.

By the time they reached home, word came over the radio that because of a minor accident at the plant, everyone should stay indoors. There was no reason for concern, no danger, but windows should be closed. Everyone should bathe. The clothes they'd worn should be disposed of.

But there was no water for bathing. It was all going to firefighting equipment that was pumping millions of gallons of water onto a raging graphite fire. All that water was going up in clouds of radioactive steam. Helicopters were dumping sandbags and lead into the reactor, throwing up tons of clouds of nuclear fuel, graphite, and vaporized lead. It rose fast in the red pillar of heat, then spiraled around as the wind changed direction. Mothers in Pripyat noticed specks of dust on their floors. When they rubbed it with their fingers, it smeared gray, the color of pencil markings.

Most people were nervous but not yet scared. There had been accidents before, plenty of them. Every once in a while, government trucks and bulldozers ripped up all the asphalt in town and carted it away. About once a month, the plant bled off radioactive steam. It was no big deal. Nothing hurt, nothing smelled bad, nobody's hair fell out or anything.

Some of the nuclear engineers from the plant, however, were getting more than nervous. They knew what radiation was and what it could do to living tissue. They could well imagine why the roads to the plant and also to Kiev were blocked. They knew why workers coming off shift from Reactor Blocks One and Two were being confined at the medical clinic.

Valentina's husband, Sergei, a nuclear physicist, started phoning around. The town medical officer said there was no problem; the only reason he hadn't sent his children to school was because they happened to have sore throats. But another doctor, risking a few years in prison for his honesty, said to spread the word that everyone should dress as if for winter and that no one should go outside. A town councilman in the Communist party said there was no problem, but it might be wise to start packing. For how long might they be gone? The party member hesitated before whispering to his friend, "Forever."

That night, they saw a horrifying red pillar of light stabbing straight up out of Reactor Number Four. They'd never seen such a color. It seemed the color of hell shining a light into the dark sky. Helicopters were flying into it, then whisking away. Sergei said that it couldn't be a regular fire. Everything would have been burned up by then. He went to warn some relatives who had no radio or telephone.

Only at 2:00 P.M. the next afternoon did the radio admit to a "trifling" accident and advise citizens to prepare for the possibility of a temporary evacuation. They should take necessary documents and enough clothes for two days. Then the word came to leave houses and apartments immediately and wait on the sidewalk. No cars would be allowed to leave the city.

As soon as everyone had left the buildings, the doors were locked behind them. No one could go back in. Everyone waited while 1,100 city buses, just driven up from Kiev, dispersed around the city.

For up to three hours, the entire population stood in an invisible shower of isotopes. The air they were breathing was radiating 10 rads per hour—close to 20 times the allowable *annual* dose for non-nuclear workers. The pavement they stood on was radiating 50 roentgens per hour. Everyone felt dizzy and nauseous, collapsing with fatigue and vomiting on the sidewalks.

As they boarded the buses, they left behind their radioactive dogs and cats. People scheduled to work at the plant had to stay, too. Valentina's husband was among them. His children, 5, 12, and 16 years old, hugged him. He said, "Forgive me. I don't know what's going to happen." When Valentina asked how long they'd be away, he said "Forever." Her face went so pale he thought she'd pass out, so he said, "Only kidding. Just two days." But he couldn't resist adding, "Or five hundred years." The youngest boy didn't want to leave his radioactive father. To get him on the radioactive bus, they had to tear him from his father's radioactive legs.

The buses headed south. Their wheels left radioactive trails down the highway. They stirred up radioactive dust. Some drove to Kiev, some to villages, some to Young Pioneer camps that had been built as summer camps for children and, if necessary, rural refuge from war. The refugees flocked to medical clinics to find out if they'd absorbed any radiation. The clinics refused to take readings. Word had come down from the Party that no information about radioactivity should be shared with anyone.

Valentina and her children ended up at a Young Pioneer camp. Like the 2,000 other refugees there, they slept in tents or underground bomb shelters. They ate in a dining hall that was stifling with the crowd of adults and children. Windows were kept closed to prevent the isotopes from floating in and contaminating the food.

It was hard to sleep at night. People who worked at the Chernobyl plant had to return once a day for a 12-hour shift. At night they coughed almost constantly, trying to expel the radionuclides from their lungs. Everyone had sore throats from the iodine 131 in their thyroids. Valentina's ankles, which the day before had waded through the foam in the streets, swelled as clots formed in their arteries. The skin on her lower legs turned a toasted brown.

Natasha, who earlier had been able to see the plant two miles away, now felt she was looking through insect eyes. Hundreds of images swirled before her, and the floor at her feet looked domed and distant. Everyone else was sick with sore throats, headaches, intestinal problems, chest pains, nausea, fatigue, faintness. No one knew exactly what was happening, and authorities were still denying any problems. While they ate in the dining hall, they watched television. They saw the Ukrainian minister of health, Anatoly Romanenko, come on and clearly state that there was no danger, no problem. All they had to do was take a few basic precautions.

Eventually, Valentina, Sergei, and their children were diagnosed as having radiation poisoning. The government sent them to a sanatorium far to the north, in Leningrad. (In 1991, the name of the city was changed to St. Petersburg.) They went in buses that had lead plates over the windows. No one was sure if it was to keep radioactivity out or in.

At the sanatorium they were checked for radiation. The readings were high, so they were told to remove their clothes. But the readings were still high, so they were ordered to shower. The readings were still high, so their hair was shaved off. The readings were still high, but there was nothing left to remove.

Doctors wouldn't come near them without putting on special masks and gloves. The patients didn't know it then, but the doctors were receiving a 25 percent bonus for handling hazardous materials. Valentina was diagnosed as having dystonia—lack of tone in blood vessels—and thrombosis—blood clots—in her legs.

Sergei, who had received higher doses of radiation as he filled sandbags for dumping on the reactor fire, had more serious problems. His skin peeled off. He had a fever so high that the hospital would not release his records. His blood pressure erratically rose and fell to dangerous levels. For the next several years his daughter would suffer from a complex of diseases. She was allergic to many things, including her own hormones. Combing her hair or scratching an itch would be enough to set off a rash and blisters.

They spent several weeks in the sanatorium and then were released. The government gave them compensation for their apartment, car, furniture, food, clothes, and other possessions that were still in Pripyat, but it wasn't enough to replace even their clothes. Sergei was unable to work. Since there was no going back to Pripyat, they had nowhere to live. They went to Kiev and stayed here and there with friends for several months until Valentina found a job. In November they and several other families were given apartments in two buildings set aside for refugees from Pripyat. Life there was uneasy. Everyone was sick, and other people in Kiev treated them as untouchable outcasts. People would not go near the buildings. They wouldn't ride in an elevator with people from Pripyat. Parents warned children that if they played with Pripyat children, they'd go bald.

Natasha lives in the same building. Her eyesight has returned to normal but she has continuing problems with her thyroid and pancreas. She also has dystonia and irregular blood pressure, as well as liver, bladder, and gastrointestinal problems. She suffers from constant fatigue and almost constant headaches. She often faints, which bothers her because it scares her children to see their mother fall unconscious. Until Ukraine became an independent country, no doctor would tell her the problems were related to radioactivity. Now they say so but have no idea how to treat her.

Glasnost

The world outside the Soviet Union knew more about what was happening than the victims it was happening to. On April 28 Sweden registered the first signs of a nuclear mishap. A monitoring station noticed rising levels of radioactivity. Further analysis revealed a bizarre array of rare isotopes, a combination not normally produced by an atomic explosion or a nuclear reactor leak. One of the isotopes was ruthenium, which melts only at 4,050°F (2,250°C)—a temperature found only on the sun, in a melting nuclear reactor, or, for an instant, in a nuclear bomb. An assessment of atmospheric conditions pointed at the Soviet Union. Sweden announced the discovery and made diplomatic inquiries to Moscow. At first Moscow admitted to nothing but later conceded a trifling accident, a quick and minor release of radioactivity.

Until the Chernobyl disaster, the Soviet Union had been secretive to the point of paranoia. Few journalists were allowed in the country except under controlled circumstances. Soviet media, controlled by the government, never admitted to a weakness, error, hazard, or inadequacy of any sort. Quite to the contrary, the Soviet press constantly extolled the superiority of Soviet progress and technology.

Soviet president Mikhail Gorbachev began to change that suppressive rule. Launching a new policy of political freedom and openness, called glasnost, the Soviet government began to allow some freedom of expression and to carefully and selectively admit facts that had once been secret.

Before Chernobyl the world wondered how serious Gorbachev was about glasnost. The explosion at Chernobyl marked a clear turning point. The disaster was too big to deny. The causes too clearly pointed to the fundamental failures of the Soviet system of government—the bureaucracy, the incompetence, the technological inferiority. Gorbachev seems to have recognized this and decided that it was time to admit the country's shortcomings—not all of them, but at least the ones it couldn't deny.

The winds over Chernobyl shifted from northwest to southwest, veering the continuing cloud down from Scandinavia into northern and central Europe. Meteorologists calculated that the radiation could only be coming from Ukraine. An American satellite focused in on Chernobyl. It showed a smear of smoke boiling from a destroyed building. Newspapers around the world reported the accident. Shortwave radio networks broadcast the news into the Soviet Union. The first news of the disaster, therefore, came from outside the country. Only on Monday, April 28, did the Kremlin issue a statement admitting to a fire at the power plant called Chernobyl.

Kiev

While the rest of the world watched in horror, two and a half million people in Kiev, just 80 miles (140 kilometers) to the south of Chernobyl, knew little if anything. Rumors were floating around, but that was not unusual in a country where the government and the press were never seen as sources of true information. In this case, no rumor could be as bad as what was really happening. No one really worried about it. By April 30, however, radiation levels were 100 times that of safe levels.

The first people to notice something amiss were at the Physics Institute of the Academy of Sciences of Ukraine. Since the institute often used radioactive materials, equipment to detect radiation monitored everyone leaving the building. That Monday, officials were surprised to find radiation coming *into* the building. It was on people's clothes. These weren't people from Chernobyl or Pripyat. They were people who had just ridden city buses to work, as they had every other morning. But this morning, April 28, the buses were radioactive. They'd been to Pripyat to pick up the evacuees. The evacuees had left so much radiation on the buses that people who sat in the seats the next morning were wearing clothes that would qualify as hazardous materials. Dosimeters showed that clothing had radiation levels five times higher than that allowed on equipment used to handle radioactive material, and thousands of times higher than that allowed to come in contact with people.

A scientist (who requests anonymity) immediately alerted the secretary of the Communist party at the institute. The secretary, a friend, told him to say nothing to anyone or he would be in big trouble. But the danger was too great to ignore. The scientist called the Civil Defense Department. They, too, told him to keep silent. He called his sister, who had children. He begged her to leave the city immediately. She brushed him off as exaggerating the danger. He exaggerated it even more—ten times more—to scare her. He found out later that even that exaggeration was still far less than the truth.

His sister did nothing at first. But over the next few days, she and other mothers noticed that the children of top Party leaders were not reporting to school. They were all taking unexpected vacations to Camp Artek, a huge Young Pioneer camp on the Black Sea, well to the south. Then she was worried. She made immediate plans to fly to Moscow with her children. Her boss, however, refused to allow her vacation days or leave of absence. Word had come down from the party. No one in Ukraine was allowed to leave his or her job.

The first public notification came on April 28, a small newspaper item of a few lines. It reported a fire at Chernobyl but said nothing of danger, radiation, or the evacuation of 45,000 people.

On April 30 the radioactive cloud reached Kiev. The government issued no warning or notification. According to Dr. Iurii Shcherbak, a physician who in 1991 became minister of the environment of Ukraine, the government knew that radiation levels were 100 times the safe level. Nevertheless, the May 1 celebrations went on as scheduled. Millions of people spent the day outdoors, enjoying the first warm days of spring.

Leonid V. Skripka, a plant biologist at the time, had heard the rumors. Friends at the Academy of Sciences told him their radiometers showed readings unbelievably high. They were finding readings of 10 curies of alpha particles per square meter—more curies than would be healthy over a square kilometer.

Skripka had seen the warning in the newspaper and knew his government well enough to see the hint of truth that appeared in the press. He also knew radiation well enough. He called home to tell his wife to call their daughter indoors, close the windows, take a shower, change clothes, and leave the dirty ones outside the house. He rushed home and called all his neighbors. No one

Residents of Kiev express shock while reading news of the Chernobyl disaster.

believed him. The blue sky, the warm sun, the light green buds on the trees—it was just too beautiful to be deadly. The television showed the parade downtown. Girls in short uniform skirts were marching down the street, their bare legs, arms, and hair soaking up the invisible radionuclides. Competitors in a long-distance international bicycle race were huffing and puffing through the radioactive air.

A technician fills a tank truck with a solution designed to decontaminate people, clothes, and equipment.

Skripka had an old Geiger counter he'd been given long ago for civil defense. Somehow he got it to work. The readings in the apartment were high. Out the window, higher still. He waved it over his daughter's hair. The needle tilted to the top end of the scale. As he and his wife cut off their daughter's hair, Skripka struggled to believe he was right and the millions of people in the streets, in the parade, in the bicycle race and outdoor games were wrong.

Over the next few days suspicion spread. A group of Japanese tourists heard the rumor, perhaps from home, and promptly fled the country. The children of Party leaders were disappearing from school. One mother recalls joking with her sister, a kindergarten teacher, that she'd be out of a job soon because her best customers were leaving. Retirees from the Party were being issued iodine pills at pharmacies, though less important people were told no iodine was available. A number of people died when they overdosed on iodine they drank straight from bottles or, worse, drank other disinfectants.

Civil defense units in factories and neighborhoods were detecting radiation. As they reported their findings, Party officials told them to keep quiet and to turn in their radiometers for "adjustment." The chief of one unit had his workers dress in special suits with respirators, but then an official from the Party told him to stop before he set off a panic.

Leonid Skripka later had access to a secret report written at the Academy of Sciences. It said that if citizens had stayed indoors during the first few hours of fallout, effects on thyroids would have been a quarter as bad as they were. If people had had iodine pills, the effects would have been one-fifteenth as bad.

People got even more suspicious when television programs made efforts to deny any problem. The few minor news reports told of a fire at the Chernobyl power plant but no danger outside the immediate area. On television, a peasant woman living near Chernobyl spoke as if an expert, explaining that she neither saw nor felt anything different, that she felt fine. Government doctors had checked her and found her radiation levels lower than normal.

The panic in Kiev started on May 5 and 6. Ironically, the radioactive plume from the fire, which was still burning, was now blowing away from Kiev. But people either didn't know this or didn't believe it. They rushed to the train stations and airports. A black market for tickets sprang up within hours. People bought tickets to anywhere outside of Kiev, even to the north, closer to the danger. The train station was probably the worst place to be.

As empty trains came into the city they pulled in clouds of radioactive dust. The trains themselves were radioactive. The crowd at the station was radioactive, with everybody radiating everybody else.

Rumors raged like the fire at the reactor and spread like the radioactive fallout. Vodka was supposed to help cleanse the body of radiation. Red wine would help, too. Plant foods rich in red pigments—beets, strawberries, cranberries—countered the effects. But you had to be careful. Strawberries supposedly tended to pick up and hold radiation. You couldn't know what you were buying. The government claimed to be monitoring food supplies, but no one believed the government anymore.

The minister of health appeared on television to vehemently deny any dangers. Radiation levels were low, he said. No one would suffer. All they had to do was take a few precautions. Stay indoors. Keep windows closed at night. Sweep out the house often. Wash their hands twice a day. Keep their pets clean.

But then, unexpectedly, a member of the Soviet parliament, Volodymyr Yavorivsky, came on and told the truth. People recognized it as truth because his version of the news was bad. He warned people not to venture outdoors, to avoid fresh foods, to flee from any place within hundreds of miles of Chernobyl. The people who saw him on television were shocked not only by the news and its seriousness but also by Yavorivsky's honesty. The truth on television! It was a first in the country's history. They feared not only for themselves but for Yavorivsky. He was probably dooming himself to a very long prison sentence. (As things turned out, in 1991 he became chairman of Ukraine's Chernobyl Commission.)

The fire at the reactor was finally doused on May 6. On May

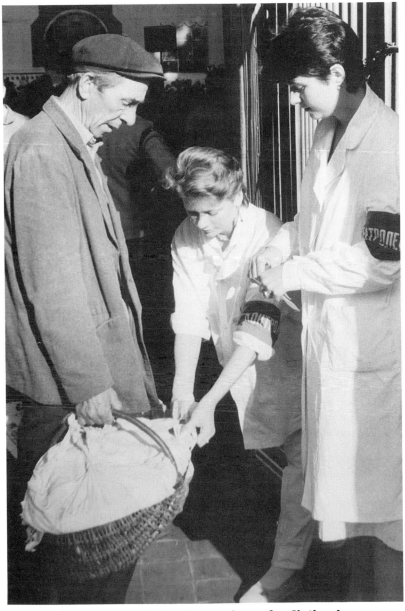

A government scientist checks for signs of radiation in produce entering a Kiev greenmarket.

14 Soviet president Mikhail Gorbachev appeared on television to explain the truth. He admitted to the explosion, the spread of radiation, the danger to people who lived near the reactor. He also spent a lot of time accusing Western countries of gloating over their supposed technical superiority. He reaffirmed that there was no danger to the general population, that food supplies were being checked, that the mess would be cleaned up.

In late May it was decided to evacuate all children from Kiev and northern Ukraine. They were loaded into trains and taken south to Camp Artek, on the Black Sea, and other Young Pioneer camps. Owing to the sudden crowd of campers, conditions were cramped, dirty, and poorly supervised. The environment was healthier than Kiev, however. Radiation was lower and clean food could be brought in from other parts of the country.

Back in Kiev, morality spiraled downward. The kids were gone. A sense of imminent doom pervaded the city. People were drinking vodka and wine in a futile, desperate effort to save their lives. They joked about how to feed a child with two heads, how to wash the radiation from your parakeet, how to iron your cat after removing it from the washing machine, how to use tweezers to pick up radionuclides from your floor. Everybody felt sick, maybe from radiation, maybe from stress, maybe from too much vodka and red wine. Men, fearing the radiation would render them impotent, were seeking sex as if it would be their last time. Women, fearing death by radiation, saw no reason not to join them. Pregnant women, fearing genetic damage, were lining up for abortions, legal or illegal. They weren't taking any chances. For all they knew, they had monsters in their wombs.

Zones of Radiation

In April 1990 the Soviet government divided the contaminated areas into four zones, each with its own restrictions and special compensations. Zone One is the 18-mile (30-kilometer) radius around the Chernobyl plant. Virtually all of the 135,000 people in this area were evacuated in the first days and weeks after the accident. This zone was ordered evacuated in the first days following the accident.

Some 200,000 have been evacuated or scheduled to be evacuated from Zones Two and Three. Zone Two is any area emitting more than 3 curies of strontium, 15 of cesium, or 0.1 of plutonium per square kilometer. Zone Two was still being evacuated in 1991. No immediate urgency was seen since the danger was in doses that would be accumulated over the course of decades.

Zone Three is any area emitting more than 0.15 curie of strontium, 5 of cesium, or 0.1 plutonium per square kilometer. The annual dose of radiation, from the environment and food, would exceed 100 millirads per year. People may still live in Zone Three, but they are not allowed to produce agricultural products or burn local firewood.

Zone Four emits more than 0.02 curie of strontium, 1 curie of cesium, or 0.01 curie of plutonium. With a few exceptions, agricultural products may be produced here. Annual doses in Zone Four are not supposed to exceed 100 millirads.

People are entitled to special benefits and compensations according to the zone where they live. Those in Zone Two, for example, receive food, water, and cooking fuel from the government until they are given somewhere else to live. They are entitled to housing in a clean area. Those in Zone Four are exempt from

The entrance to Zone One, the restricted area around the Chernobyl plant

income taxes. Everyone receives monetary compensation, though it is very low. People call it "coffin money" because it amounts to just about enough to bury them once the radiation finishes its work.

To receive these benefits, people want to have their area classified as a zone with a lower number. Because of vague wording in the law, a given area can receive the classification of an adjacent area because food products tend to cross the lines as one village sells crops to another. A cow doesn't necessarily know which side of a field is in a more radioactive zone, and the farmer doesn't necessarily care. Besides, the lines shift when the wind blows radioactive dust from one zone to another, and rain washes contaminated soil downhill. In 1989, 20 major Belorussian farm cooperatives had to be closed due to high levels of radioactivity. As late as November 1991 a farming cooperative just outside Zone One was closed, ostensibly for the same reason. Until that time the farm had been shipping milk, potatoes, and wheat to Kiev.

Regardless of where the boundaries lie, the rules have been ignored to some extent. One hundred elderly people still live within the Prohibited Zone near the plant. People in Zone Two still raise crops because the government doesn't deliver enough food. Inevitably, some of the crops end up on dinner tables in Kiev, Minsk, and Moscow.

A major issue is whether Kiev is within a contaminated zone. The government of Ukraine says it is not. The government of Kiev, however, has evidence that every point in the city qualifies as Zone Four, and a few "hot spots" should be in Zone Three. The problem is that if the city is included in Zone Four, 2.6 million people will be exempted from income taxation. The government of Ukraine, already economically strapped, would lose a major source of revenue. If all these people were exempt from taxes and entitled to special benefits and compensation, the government treasury would soon be empty. The few public services that still work would shut down, and several hundred thousand victims of Chernobyl would see the end of their "coffin money" before they are ready for the coffin.

A German firefighter cleans contaminated dirt from a car entering the country from Poland.

CHAPTER SIX

· · · · · · · · · · · · · · · · ·

Global
Chernobyl

The radioactive cloud that rose from the ruins of the Chernobyl reactor has circled the earth several times. Gradually its radionuclides are settling to the land and sea to enter the planetary ecosystem.

The most intense concentrations blew across the areas nearest Chernobyl and then into Scandinavia and Europe. Europeans were on the edge of panic as information trickled out of the Soviet Union. The press reported worsening scenarios and often contradicted one another. News reports in Austria at first said the radioactivity would not affect Austrians, but by May 1 the government was advising people to avoid drinking rainwater, to wash fresh vegetables carefully, and not to let children play in sandboxes. By May 7 the government was saying that although there was no danger, the sale of milk and fresh vegetables was prohibited and that children and pregnant women should avoid contact with the ground. By June 17 levels of cesium 137 were twice the allowable level in pork and four times the level in rabbits. The Austrian government recommended that cows not be allowed to graze in pastures unless the grass there had been mowed at least twice. Arguing that radiation could not be mowed away, people avoided all meat and dairy products.

Map of Europe at the time of the Chernobyl explosion

In Greece, police broke up riots as people panicked to buy canned food and bottled water in supermarkets. The Greek Orthodox church condemned the use of nuclear power. In Italy, a poll revealed that 70 percent of Italians were against nuclear energy, and 100,000 people demonstrated against it in Rome. In Denmark, a civil defense unit made radiation checks on all persons, vehicles, and boats coming from eastern Europe or the Baltic Sea. People were advised to stay indoors if it rained. In Germany, farmers were advised to keep their cows indoors whether it rained or not. Several Germans were hospitalized after

Protestors in Berlin dump containers of milk and other foods contaminated by radiation fallout from the Chernobyl explosion.

drinking iodine. The government insisted that there was no danger although in some places radiation levels were 500 times higher than normal background levels. A riot at a nuclear reprocessing plant left 157 police and 200 demonstrators injured.

In France, the government spent a week denying the presence of any significant levels of radiation in French territory. The cloud seemed to have stopped at the borders, as if denied an entry visa. Food grown on the German side of the French border was banned, but food grown on French soil was supposedly uncontaminated. Only on May 10 did the director of a nuclear safety agency reveal that levels in some areas were 400 times higher than normal. Sixty-three percent of French people did not trust the reports issued by their government.

In northern Sweden, lichen, which gets its nutrients directly from the air, soaked up extremely large quantities of radionuclides. The 700,000 Lapps who live in northern Scandinavia were especially endangered. Their reindeer, which live on lichen and provide the Lapps with most of their food, clothing, transportation, and implements, became highly contaminated. Meat from 50,000 reindeer had to be disposed of. The government raised the permissible levels of cesium 137 in food for Lapps so that they could continue their nomadic life-style. The only alternative was to move them all to the city, effectively destroying a culture that had lived in the Arctic tundra for more than 10,000 years.

Seven years later, Turkey opened an investigation of unusual health problems among its population near the Black Sea. An earlier study had indicated that some 100,000 people may have been affected by fallout from Chernobyl. The Turkish Union of Doctors was charging the government with "failure to take necessary precautions to protect public health." The charges were based on a sharp increase in miscarriages, stillborn babies, deformed babies, and cancer victims.

Death in the United States

Chernobyl's huge radioactive cloud arrived on the west coast of the United States on May 5. Federal and state governments assured everyone that there was no danger. Levels of radioactivity were well within limits considered acceptable. It would not be necessary to wash vegetables, avoid milk, or stay indoors.

Actually, the government had no reason to suspect danger. Research had shown that such low levels of radiation were safe. But the research was based on the effects observed in relatively low numbers of people or people subjected to the intense burst of radiation from the two atomic bombs exploded over Japan. It was difficult to draw accurate conclusions that would apply to a situation involving slow, steady radiation. Thanks to the explosion at Chernobyl, however, American scientists now had their first chance to collect health and mortality statistics on the U.S. population of more than 200 million who were exposed to low doses of radiation.

Jay M. Gould, a fellow of the Institute for Policy Studies in Washington, D.C., analyzed statistics comparing mortality and radiation levels. His conclusions were very disturbing. He found that in May 1986, the total number of deaths in the United States rose 5.3 percent over that of May 1985. The death rate in June, July, and August was also significantly higher, though it quickly declined in succeeding months. The death rate rose most among AIDS patients, people with infectious diseases, infants, and the elderly—in other words, people whose immune systems were already weak. The odds of an increase that large occurring just by chance were a million to one. There had to be a cause.

An interesting intersection of statistics pointed an accusatory finger even more directly at Chernobyl. Gould found that the death rate increased most in regions that showed the highest levels of iodine 131 in milk. It could be assumed that levels of other radionuclides were also probably higher in those regions. Levels of iodine 131 were lowest in the region around Texas, where the least rain had fallen, and the death rate there remained unchanged from the year before.

Most horrifying was the increase in infant mortality. In the United States as a whole, the rate in June 1986 was 12.3 percent higher than in June of the year before. In the South Atlantic region, the rate was 28 percent higher.

Marvin Lavenhar, director of the Division of Biostatistics and Epidemiology at New Jersey Medical School in Newark, said, "You can't escape the fact that something happened in the summer of 1986. . . . We are looking for other factors [besides Chernobyl] and so far we can't find any explanation."

Radiation experts questioned the link between Chernobyl and the increase in mortality. The rise in radiation in the United States was a tiny fraction of normal background radiation and well within levels considered safe. It was odd that in Europe, where radiation levels were 100 to 1,000 times higher than in the United States, statistics did not reveal similar increases.

Statisticians also questioned the validity of Gould's findings. An official at the Vital Records Unit of the Washington State Department of Social and Health Services said that in his state, where Gould found the highest increase in mortality, the death rate in the summer months had been rising every year since 1983. He also said the increase was not as high as Gould had reported, and that infant mortality had in fact *decreased* by 5 percent compared to the previous summer.

In a shockingly accusatorial book, *Deadly Deceit*, Gould and coauthor Benjamin A. Goldman said that government statistics on the birth rates in California and Massachusetts had mysteriously changed. Until the end of 1986 the statistics showed an increase in infant mortality just after Chernobyl. But the figures for total births were adjusted upward at the end of the year. The adjustments, said Gould and Goldman, began in May 1986. By increasing the number of births but not the number of infant deaths, the statistics produced a radically *lower* rate of infant mortality. The book also showed evidence of similar adjustments in Pennsylvania and Maryland just after the nuclear accident at Three Mile Island.

According to information in *Deadly Deceit*, infant mortality also soared in Germany. In the most heavily contaminated regions it rose 68 percent. The rate was much less steep in the least contaminated regions.

The total number of deaths in the United States during the summer months of 1986 was about 16,000 higher than during those months in the year before Chernobyl. Unquestionably other causes, including the general increase in population, the increase in the average age of the population, and the AIDS epidemic contributed to the increase in total deaths. But these factors cannot account for the coincidental leap in mortality just after Chernobyl and the decline a few months later. Although scientists cannot establish a clear cause-and-effect link between the slight increase in radiation and the staggering increase in deaths, it seems very possible that several thousand Americans might be included among the victims of Chernobyl.

Chernobyl's Effect on Nature

In the past, before the days of high technology, coal miners used to take a canary into the mine with them. If the canary suddenly died, it indicated the presence of gases that would kill the miners, too, if they didn't leave immediately.

Birds may have given us a similar warning about the presence of something deadly in the United States in the summer of

1986. An ornithologist, Dr. David F. DeSante, noticed a radical decrease in bird population in northern California, Oregon, and Washington. Until June 8 it seemed that the bird population was about 12 percent above normal. But by mid-June the population seemed to have dropped to 56 percent of normal. By late July it was merely 24 percent of normal. DeSante first suspected herbicides or insecticides, but a little investigation revealed no change in the local use of such chemicals. Then he remembered that it had rained when the radiation from Chernobyl had passed over the region in the first week of May.

DeSante's information closely matched that noticed by other ornithologists. Virtually all species of birds were affected, but two weren't: woodpeckers and swallows. Their salvation, apparently, was in their diet. Woodpeckers eat insects that live on rotten wood—wood that does not bring up rainwater from the soil. Swallows eat insects that breed in streams, where they consume rotted vegetation. The species that died most were those which eat insects and caterpillars that lived off fresh vegetation—a source of radioactivity in a recently radioactive environment. As the insects ate radiated vegetation, they concentrated the radiation. The birds then ate these concentrated doses and soon died or failed to reproduce. Radiation was seen as even more likely when research in other areas of the country showed that bird populations decreased most in regions that had the highest concentrations of iodine 131 in milk. The iodine arrived in the milk via the grass that the cows ate, an indication of the general presence of radioactivity in vegetation.

In 1992 scientists found that the radiation had flown about as far as it could go. In a snow pit 23.5 miles (38 kilometers) from the South Pole, geochemists took a sample of snow that had lain in layers for several years. It showed raised levels of radiation for the years 1955 through 1974, when atomic bombs were still tested in the atmosphere. The radiation level rose again, to 20 to 30 times normal background levels, in late 1987 and 1988—about the time that winds from Ukraine could have reached that area. Inexplicably, snow in other areas did not show the raised levels.

It would be quite difficult, if not impossible, to accurately determine how Chernobyl's 50 tons of radioactive materials have affected or will affect the earth's ecosystem. The radionuclides are blowing around the atmosphere, washing into the sea, seeping into groundwater, lingering in the leaves and wood of plants, flying hither and yon in the bodies of insects and birds. During the lifetime of the radioactivity—hundreds of thousands of years— the uncountable billions of billions of particles will spread all over the planet. They have already entered the food chain and are being passed from plant to insect to bird to fish to mammal and, inevitably, to humans.

Biologists are concerned that the widespread radioactivity may cause mutations in a virus or bacteria, turning it dangerous or even deadly. They have a wary eye on Lyme disease, which is caused by a bacteria that was harmless to humans before 1975. The disease first appeared around Lyme, Connecticut, a few miles from the Millstone nuclear power plant. Millstone has leaked more radiation than any other U.S. nuclear power plant besides Three Mile Island, and in 1975 alone released some three million curies. Some scientists suspect, though by no means can they prove, that there may be a link between the increased radiation and the sudden mutation.

CHAPTER SEVEN

·······················

The Politics of Radiation

Thexplosion at Chernobyl left the planet with the biggest mess humankind has ever made. Unlike the messes left by earthquakes, volcanoes, tidal waves, and wars, this one cannot be cleaned up. Unless some unforeseen technology finds a way to sweep up the isotopes and somehow convert them to harmless atoms, Chernobyl's radioactivity will probably outlive civilization. We are as far from the last half-life of plutonium as we are from our semihuman ancestors who had not yet learned to make fire.

Given the seriousness of the problem—the thousands of lives at stake, the billions of dollars involved—it is only natural for blame to fly wild and clues to the truth to be hidden, distorted, and destroyed. The first official attempt came from Anatoly Ivanovich Mayorets, Soviet minister of energy and electrification. On July 18, 1986, he issued written instructions forbidding anyone in his ministry to release information to the press.

Official denials of the truth, however, are not completely necessary. Given the nature of the truth—the invisibility of the isotopes, their unknown effects on the human body—it is hard to know when truth has been found, and very easy to mold vague information to fit ulterior motives. All too often the claims and opinions of people, governments, agencies, companies, scientists, doctors, and victims seem suspiciously in line with their own self-interest.

Soviet Press Reports

By Soviet standards, the government-controlled press of the Soviet Union was surprisingly quick and honest in reporting the accident at Chernobyl. In the past, major nuclear catastrophes, including one at Chelyabinsk in 1957-1958, were never announced.

By Western standards, however, the reports in the Soviet press would be considered criminally negligent. Although authorities very quickly had a general idea of the seriousness of the explosion and the extent of radioactive contamination, very little appeared in the press, and what appeared was late, inaccurate, and designed to deny the full truth.

The first Soviet report was issued at 8:00 P.M. on April 28, two days after the explosion. It referred to an "accident" and said that measures were being taken to eliminate consequences. There was no mention of radiation. This report came only after Sweden had detected the radiation and pinpointed its source.

On April 29 a television news program reported that two people had died in the accident, part of the reactor building had been destroyed, and four towns were being evacuated. There was no mention of radiation.

The first mention of radiation came on April 30. Radiation levels were reported to be decreasing, and 197 people were reported hospitalized.

The news on May 1 and 2 focused on the May Day celebrations. Secondary reports mentioned the accident but offered evidence that it was not serious. Radiation levels in the surrounding area were reported to be *lower* than usual. Peasants were interviewed on television. They said they felt fine and everything seemed normal.

Over the next few days the government released more information on the accident and evacuation of Pripyat. Nothing indicated danger from radiation. On May 7, TASS, the Soviet news agency, reported that many Kiev residents were trying to leave the city. *Pravda*, a Moscow daily newspaper, reported that radiation levels in Ukraine, Belorussia, and Russia were within international safety standards.

On May 9, Hans Blix, director general of the International Atomic Energy Agency (IAEA) held a press conference at which he said that the situation in Kiev was normal and that radiation at the edge of the 18-mile (30-kilometer) zone had been 10 to 15 millirems on April 26 but had dropped to 0.15 millirem, well within safety limits. The Ukrainian newspaper *Pravda Ukrainy* offered the first advice on how to protect against the effects of radiation. Anatoly Romanenko, Ukrainian minister of health, stated that the major problem was dust. For the first time *Pravda* in Moscow admitted that radiation levels had risen, though not to dangerous levels.

On May 12 an article in *Izvestia*, the government-issued daily newspaper, said that radiation in drinking water in Kiev was being reported to the public every morning. Current levels were in the normal range. With Orwellian simplicity, however, "normal" had been revised upward from 0.5 rem per year to 10 rems per year so that at current rates, a dangerous dose would now take five years instead of two months to accumulate.

On May 15 all Soviet newspapers carried Gorbachev's speech of the day before. He attacked the West for criticizing Soviet technology even though the *Challenger* space shuttle had just exploded, but admitted that "for the first time ever we encountered in reality such a sinister force as nuclear energy that has escaped control." He also said that as soon as the government had had reliable data, it had announced it to the Soviet people and foreign governments.

A UN Report: Scientific Fact or Political Fiction?

The explosion at Chernobyl destroyed more than a nuclear power plant. It also destroyed what little faith the people of the Soviet Union had in their government. After the government studied the radioactive conditions and health consequences in contaminated regions, few people believed the results. Millions of people complained that they lived in radioactive areas and their health was suffering. They wanted clean food, new housing, special health care, and monetary compensation. The results of the Soviet studies, however, indicated that there were no serious problems in the contaminated areas that had not been evacuated. Inevitably, people accused the government of corruption and political maneuvering. It certainly wouldn't be the first time in that country.

In hopes of gaining credibility, the Soviet government invited the United Nations to verify its information and conclusions. In 1989 the UN IAEA was given the task.

The primary question was whether people still living in contaminated areas could continue to live there safely. The project did not assess conditions in the Prohibited Zone around the Chernobyl plant or check the health of the 600,000 liquidators or the over 200,000 people who had been evacuated to uncontaminated areas.

The team of 200 doctors, radiologists, nutritionists, psychologists, and other specialists came from 23 countries. They worked with the tremendous amount of radiological and medical information that the government of the Soviet Union had gathered. To verify its accuracy, they selected a sample of 28 (out of 2,000) heavily contaminated cities and villages for detailed surveys of people, soil, water, air, animals, and foods. For purposes of comparison, they performed similar surveys of seven towns with little or no contamination.

The Soviet government had decided that a lifetime dose of 35 rems was acceptable. In areas where people would receive more than that, or where radiation exceeded 40 curies per square kilometer, people should be evacuated. Elsewhere, people could continue to live at least temporarily. The IAEA was asked to determine if that 35-rems "safe living" level was really safe, and whether Soviet studies had accurately predicted how much radiation people would likely absorb in their lifetimes.

The team tested soil, water, and food to verify Soviet radiation readings. They had a number of residents wear dosimeter badges that would register radiation wherever they went. Some 8,000 people were analyzed to see how much cesium they had absorbed. Many thousands of people were given thorough health checkups.

After seven months of investigation, the IAEA concluded that in general the Soviet methods of assessment were scientifically sound. In fact, the report said, Soviet estimates of radiation levels and doses tended to be higher than those found by the IAEA. Only 10 percent of the residents who wore dosimeter badges in highly contaminated areas registered enough radiation for the badge to measure.

Though many health problems were found, none could be directly attributed to radiation. The team found no significant increase in thyroid problems, cancer, immune deficiency, or birth defects. A major factor in the generally poor health of people in the region was probably due to *fear* of radiation, not radiation itself. Most adults in contaminated areas believed their health

Although most people have been evacuated from Zone One, a few people continue trying to earn a living there.

Although the government has prohibited using the land around Chernobyl for agricultural purposes, the people who live there must grow their own food, since little is available to buy.

was suffering because of radiation, and 83 percent of them felt the government should relocate them to an uncontaminated area.

The IAEA acknowledged serious limitations in the data provided by the Soviets. The equipment and methods they used to collect data made it difficult to compare Soviet data with that collected by the IAEA team. Nevertheless, the IAEA felt confident enough to conclude that, excluding evacuees and liquidators (close to a million people) there were *no* aftereffects from the accident. Food was clean, radiation low, public health unaffected. Even in highly contaminated areas of over 40 curies per square kilometer, radiation was hurting no one. Delayed health effects such as cancer and birth defects would be difficult to discern because they would be so rare. There was no need for further evacuation. The report said, "The . . . lifetime dose that could be potentially averted by relocation, prompted by either the 35 rems or 40 curies per square kilometer criterion, are [the same as] or less than the doses due to average natural background radiation."

In other words, even the bright red zones on radiation maps were no more dangerous than the natural radiation found anywhere else in the Soviet Union. Moving people out of these zones would do them little if any good. In fact, the report recommended less extensive restrictions on food and the need for evacuation. It was these restrictions that were causing the "radiophobia" and stress that may have led to many of the health problems in contaminated areas.

The report did little to build people's confidence. It seemed only to spread accusations of corruption to an international level. The conclusion that 50 tons of radioactive fuel could be spread around the countryside without hurting anyone seemed preposterous. A spokesman for the Chernobyl Union said that the report virtually certified that a nuclear war could be conducted safely.

Doctors, scientists, government officials, and common citizens criticized the report on several counts. They claimed that the IAEA was not impartial because it is financed by the nuclear power industry, which allegedly wanted to minimize the truth about the dangers of nuclear power. In fact, the IAEA was formed with the specific purpose of *promoting* the safe expansion of nuclear energy. Critics also claimed that the IAEA actually inspected only a few areas, and only areas for which they were given figures by the same Soviet government that had allegedly tried to hide the truth in the first place. All the IAEA did was check a small fraction of the Soviet figures and look over the rest to merely confirm that they seemed to have been calculated accurately.

Doctors also questioned IAEA reports of no increase in cancer. Leukemia and other forms of cancer occur only several years after exposure to radiation. It was only natural that a study done just five years after the accident would find no increase in rates of cancer. To give the area a clean bill of health so soon, said critics, was to condemn thousands to grave illness.

One leader in the post-Soviet Ukrainian government said that the IAEA report was "a script that had already been written" before its investigation started. He also added, "If by some chance it was not, no one will believe it anyway."

Another UN Report: Another Conclusion

In 1992, the United Nations World Health Organization performed a much smaller investigation that turned up much grimmer results. The study looked only for thyroid cancer among children in Belorussia, and it found it. In the area closest to Chernobyl, incidence was 80 times normal.

Medical professionals were especially dismayed by the deadliness of the cancers. While cancer of the thyroid can usually be "cured" by removing the thyroid gland and giving the patient doses of hormones for the rest of his or her life, one seven year old had died and ten other children were in serious condition.

The cancer was also appearing sooner than would have been predicted by the data from Hiroshima and Nagasaki. Doctors had not been expecting much increase for another few years.

Conflicting Interests

The lack of reliable data and consistent conclusions is due, in part, to a convergence of conflicting interests. No one has a good body of solid information, but various parties have bits of the truth. In the process of converting half-truths into conclusions, however, motives can come to carry more weight than mere facts.

Following the accident, the Soviet government had every reason to suppress the truth. As a failure of Soviet technology, it implied a failure in the Communist system. As a major accident, it would lay blame on a lot of people in the Communist party, from the highest Soviet leaders to the lowest functionary bureaucrats.

A once-a-week delivery inside Zone One provides the people with small quantities of bread.

And after the blame would come demands for compensation of victims and punishment for the guilty. Not many people in positions of power wanted the world to know exactly what had happened.

At first the Soviet government denied that anything had exploded. Then it denied the release of radiation. Then it denied the extent of the release. Then it denied the danger of the radiation. Then it denied the number of deaths. Then it ordered the manipulation of medical records. Then it ordered silence from anyone who knew anything. Then it offered statistical information that might have minimized (or possibly exaggerated) the extent of contamination. Then it minimized the consequences for public health. Then it disappeared, and with it went a lot of information, good or bad.

The government of Ukraine, first as a Soviet republic and then as an independent state, wanted the Soviet government to compensate Ukrainians for the damage to their land, water, and health. To press their claim, Ukraine offered data on contamination and health problems. It was quite different from that claimed by the Soviets. The Soviets used the report from the IAEA to justify its claims that damages were not as extensive as Ukraine alleged.

Before anything could be decided, Ukraine became an independent state. The Soviet government ceased to exist, and the new state of Russia came into being. Could Russia be held responsible for Soviet negligence? The question was moot because the Russian economy was virtually bankrupt and not about to send money to Ukrainians. What little was promised to the victims of Chernobyl would no longer be delivered.

Many people say that foreign aid has not been of much help,

either. With the corrupt bureaucracy of the old Communist party still intact, foreign aid tends to disappear before it reaches its intended beneficiaries. Aid from the United Nations Educational, Scientific, and Cultural Organization (UNESCO) was almost totally lost as it filtered through the bureaucracy in Moscow. Fifty million yen from Japan never came out of that same filter. A donation of coffee from Brazil went into the filter and came out in the black market. A load of vitamins went into the filter and later came out of the mouths of bureaucrats who got sick after gobbling several jars of capsules. A telethon broadcast across the Soviet Union raised millions of rubles for victims but apparently it all went to finance the building of the sarcophagus. Some cynical citizens say they wish the foreign aid would stop because it only makes the bureaucrats richer and more entrenched in their positions.

In the last few days of 1991, control of the Chernobyl facility passed into Ukrainian hands and became a Ukrainian problem. Ukrainians were delighted because it meant they could shut down the last two of the four reactors. The complete shutdown had been scheduled for 1995. When a fire destroyed the roof of the Number Two reactor hall in October 1991, however, the Ukrainians became more nervous. A few weeks later, after another fire, this time in corroded cables in Reactor One, the Ukrainians decided to move the date ahead to 1993. Many people, however, expected the shutdown to be delayed because Ukraine needed the electric power, and some 18,000 people needed their jobs at the Chernobyl plant. In 1992 Reactor One was still running and Reactor Three was restarted.

Ukrainians were less delighted to face the question of who was going to compensate the victims of Chernobyl. Tens of thousands of liquidators were living on pensions. More than 100,000 evacuees would soon be eligible for early retirement. More and more people were falling ill. A quarter of the country's farmland was too contaminated to use. The government needed more money than ever before, and the economy was collapsing. A free enterprise economic system was gradually developing, but not nearly as fast as the old centrally controlled system was disintegrating.

The federal government of Ukraine came into conflict with the municipal government of Kiev. Municipal officials in Kiev claimed that the entire city was contaminated enough to qualify as Zone Four. This entitled 2.6 million people to a number of special benefits and compensation. Most crucially, they would be exempt from paying income tax—a drop in revenues the country could ill afford. The relationship between Ukraine and Kiev became quite like that between Russia and Ukraine. Just as Russia had denied that Ukraine was dangerously contaminated, Ukraine denied that Kiev was contaminated. A detailed reassessment of radioactivity across the country is expected to clarify—and also heat up—the issue.

More Chernobyls Ahead?

At an IAEA conference in late 1992, senior Russian officials said that their country would continue to operate its 15 RBMK reactors. Although Western experts have condemned the RBMK design as inherently dangerous, the Russians said that their national economy was too fragile to suffer the loss of a major source of power.

All of the 60 nuclear reactors in the former Soviet Union and eastern Europe have safety problems. According to the IAEA, 26 of them have "serious" problems and 14 have "considerable" safety deficiencies. In 1991 there were 172 "incidents" at Russian reactors, and in 1992 there were 205. More than 100 incidents struck the five Ukrainian atomic power stations, including several at Chernobyl. An "incident" is defined as any sort of irregularity or unexpected problem, though none of those reported in 1992 were serious except for a quick leak at a plant near St. Petersburg.

In January of 1993, when melting snow leaked through the roof of an electric station 100 feet from Reactor One, shorting out a switch box and starting a fire, a spokesperson said it was no more serious than a burned-out light bulb. To bystanders, however, it looked more like a central power station billowing with acrid black smoke being fought by firefighters in gas masks. During the fire no one was sure what the shorted wires were supposed to be controlling in the reactor. Chernobyl officials were quick to point out that they had seen no need to shut down the reactors during the emergency.

Within a week another fire broke out, this time inside the sarcophagus. Some wood left inside during construction had burst into flames for no apparent reason.

Within a week after that, an oil tube burst in the turbine powered by Reactor Three, spraying oil into the turbine room. Workers were quick to spot the problem and prevent the oil from igniting.

The largest reactors in the world, two RBMKs in Lithuania, are a disaster waiting to happen. Russia will no longer reprocess spent fuel from the plants, so the fuel is being stored in pools of cooling water under the plant. Because the plant was poorly constructed, with much of its cement stolen before construction, the pools are rumored to be leaking, and the pillars that hold the reactor above them are threatening to collapse.

A shut-down reactor in the former Soviet republic of Armenia threatened to leak in 1993 when the entire country lost its power supply after a pipeline explosion cut off its supply of natural gas. Although not operating, the plant needed electricity to cool its fuel and nuclear waste. The only solution was to start up the plant once again—on very short notice—so it could generate the power it needed to remain stable. The plant had been closed after a severe earthquake damaged it in 1988.

The official U.S. response to the claims of safety problems has been to call for shutting down the reactors as soon as possible and to do nothing to prolong their use. Russian and European technical experts, however, say this solution is impractical. It would be wiser, they say, to finance the installation of safety features and overhauls of the reactors.

In January, 1993 seven of the world's leading industrial nations agreed to raise $700 million to finance an ongoing program to improve the safety of ex-Soviet reactors. The first work would be on 16 Chernobyl-type RBMK reactors and 10 other aging reactors of similar design.

Meanwhile, Russia decided to go ahead with plans to build more reactors. None had been constructed since the Chernobyl incident. Three were to be completed by 1995, and several more by 2010. One would be of the RBMK design.

By 1992 some safety features had already been installed on existing reactors. They now use a more highly enriched fuel, which will help prevent runaway chain reactions. "Scram" buttons have been installed so that operators can shut down a reactor easily and without holding their finger on a button for a minute and a half. Also, the boron control rods have been redesigned so that when their tips enter the core, they do not cause a temporary increase in power. They can now be inserted into the core in 2.5 seconds rather than the 19 seconds required before.

Still, the water and steam system inside the core is considered "a plumber's nightmare" that can easily break down and explode. Checking the condition of the piping is very difficult. The design still requires the careful and tricky balance of water, steam, and reactivity. The reactors still do not have containment structures around them that could retain leaks or the debris of an explosion. The reactors still vent radioactive gases into the atmosphere.

For these and similar reasons, the environmental watchdog organization Greenpeace says that the world has not seen its last nuclear nightmare. According to that organization, we face a 50–50 chance of another nuclear disaster of Chernobyl proportions within the next decade.

Chernobyl Today

The steel-and-concrete sarcophagus still stands around the ruins of Reactor Four. Somehow it must remain intact for the next several thousand years. Much of the fuel that melted poured into the basement of the building. No one has actually seen it—to go anywhere near it would result in instant death. A photograph shows it to resemble a giant elephant's foot standing on the floor.

Much of the fuel and other radioactive debris is scattered

throughout the hundreds of offices, corridors, closets, and other rooms of the building. This is a problem. As rain leaks in through the roof, it dissolves the radionuclides and washes them downward. Bit by bit they accumulate in certain places. The only way to find these places is to drill through several walls and insert a probe—a long, tedious, dangerous, and unreliable process. The danger is that radioactive material could build up in one place until it reaches critical mass and starts a chain reaction. In fact, according to Iurri Shcherbak, minister of the environment of Ukraine, radioactivity readings indicated such a reaction was under way in July of 1991. Fortunately, workers were able to find the place and to pump in chemicals to stop the reaction. Shcherbak now says they are "*almost* absolutely positive" that such an event cannot happen again. If it did, of course, the further destruction of Reactor Four and the likely destruction of the other three reactors would dwarf the first Chernobyl accident.

The sarcophagus was built under extreme duress—very quickly by untrained workers who were often more interested in surviving than doing a top-notch job. As with virtually everything constructed in the Soviet Union, standards were probably low. Rain is leaking in through cracks in the roof and leaking out through cracks in the floor. No one is certain that a wall could not collapse inward, sending up a cloud of radioactive dust. A minor earthquake could do the trick.

Even if the sarcophagus holds up, it was built to last only 30 years, and by 1993 Ukrainian authorities were saying it wouldn't last until the end of the decade. Before then, either another sarcophagus will need to be built—a task that could cost over a billion dollars—or the radioactive fuel and debris will have to be somehow processed and safely buried—a task considered virtually impossible with current technology.

Meanwhile, some 42.2 million cubic feet (1.2 million cubic meters) of radioactive waste in 800 storage tanks near the plant need to be monitored continuously. Just like the sarcophagus, they will need to be maintained in good condition for the next several tens of thousands of years.

Further Reading

Committee on the Biological Effects of Ionizing Radiation. *Health Effects of Exposure to Low Levels of Ionizing Radiation—BEIR V.* Washington, D.C.: National Academy Press, 1990.

Flavin, Christopher. *Reassessing Nuclear Power: The Fallout from Chernobyl.* Washington, D.C.: Worldwatch Institute, 1987.

Ford, Daniel. *Three Mile Island—Thirty Minutes to Meltdown.* New York: Penguin Books, 1982.

Gale, Robert Peter and Thomas Hauser. *Final Warning: The Legacy of Chernobyl.* New York: Warner Books, 1988.

Gould, Jay M., and Benjamin A. Goldman. *Deadly Deceit.* New York: Four Walls Eight Windows, 1991.

Hall, Eric J. *Radiation and Life.* Elmsford, N.Y.: Pergamon Press, 1984.

Marples, David R. *Chernobyl and Nuclear Powers in the USSR.* New York: St. Martin's Press, 1986.

McGovern, Brian. *Chernobyl.* San Diego: Lucent Books, 1990.

Medvedev, Grigori. *The Truth About Chernobyl.* New York: Basic Books, 1991.

Medvedev, Zhores. *The Legacy of Chernobyl.* New York: W. W. Norton and Co., 1990.

Mould, Richard F. *Chernobyl—The Real Story.* Elmsford, N.Y.: Pergamon Press, 1988.

Shcherbak, Iurri. *Chernobyl: A Documentary Story.* New York: St. Martin's Press, 1989.

Index